Current
CONTROVERSIES

Medical Marijuana

Other Books in the Current Controversies Series

Medical Marijuana

Noël Merino, Book Editor

GREENHAVEN PRESS
A part of Gale, Cengage Learning

GALE
CENGAGE Learning™

Detroit • New York • San Francisco • New Haven, Conn • Waterville, Maine • London

GALE
CENGAGE Learning™

Christine Nasso, *Publisher*
Elizabeth Des Chenes, *Managing Editor*

© 2011 Greenhaven Press, a part of Gale, Cengage Learning

Gale and Greenhaven Press are registered trademarks used herein under license.

For more information, contact:
Greenhaven Press
27500 Drake Rd.
Farmington Hills, MI 48331-3535
Or you can visit our Internet site at gale.cengage.com

For product information and technology assistance, contact us at

Gale Customer Support, 1-800-877-4253
For permission to use material from this text or product, submit all requests online at www.cengage.com/permissions

Further permissions questions can be emailed to permissionrequest@cengage.com

Articles in Greenhaven Press anthologies are often edited for length to meet page requirements. In addition, original titles of these works are changed to clearly present the main thesis and to explicitly indicate the author's opinion. Every effort is made to ensure that Greenhaven Press accurately reflects the original intent of the authors. Every effort has been made to trace the owners of copyrighted material.

Cover image copyright © Juan Camilo Bernal/Shutterstock.com.

LIBRARY OF CONGRESS CATALOGING-IN-PUBLICATION DATA

Medical marijuana / Noël Merino, book editor.
    p. cm. -- (Current controversies)
    Includes bibliographical references and index.
    ISBN 978-0-7377-5424-7 (hbk.) -- ISBN 978-0-7377-5425-4 (pbk.)
    1. Marijuana--Therapeutic use. I. Merino, Noël.
    RM666.C266M433 2011
    615'.7827--dc22
                                                            2010048167

Printed in the United States of America
1 2 3 4 5 6 7 15 14 13 12 11

Contents

Chapter 1: Should Marijuana Be a Medical Option?

Yes: Marijuana Should Be a Medical Option

No: Marijuana Should Not Be a Medical Option

Marijuana in its crude, natural form cannot meet the scientific and legal standards of a medicine and must be treated as other raw products in the development of a standardized medicine.

Chapter 2: Is Medical Marijuana Dangerous?

Outrageous claims are made about the dangers of marijuana despite the research that disputes many claims about the harms said to result from marijuana use.

Chapter 3: Should Marijuana Use Be Regulated by the Government?

Chapter 4: What Are the Effects of State Medical Marijuana Laws?

Foreword

By definition, controversies are "discussions of questions in which opposing opinions clash" (Webster's Twentieth Century Dictionary Unabridged). Few would deny that controversies are a pervasive part of the human condition and exist on virtually every level of human enterprise. Controversies transpire between individuals and among groups, within nations and between nations. Controversies supply the grist necessary for progress by providing challenges and challengers to the status quo. They also create atmospheres where strife and warfare can flourish. A world without controversies would be a peaceful world; but it also would be, by and large, static and prosaic.

The Series' Purpose

The purpose of the Current Controversies series is to explore many of the social, political, and economic controversies dominating the national and international scenes today. Titles selected for inclusion in the series are highly focused and specific. For example, from the larger category of criminal justice, Current Controversies deals with specific topics such as police brutality, gun control, white collar crime, and others. The debates in Current Controversies also are presented in a useful, timeless fashion. Articles and book excerpts included in each title are selected if they contribute valuable, long-range ideas to the overall debate. And wherever possible, current information is enhanced with historical documents and other relevant materials. Thus, while individual titles are current in focus, every effort is made to ensure that they will not become quickly outdated. Books in the Current Controversies series will remain important resources for librarians, teachers, and students for many years.

In addition to keeping the titles focused and specific, great care is taken in the editorial format of each book in the series. Book introductions and chapter prefaces are offered to provide background material for readers. Chapters are organized around several key questions that are answered with diverse opinions representing all points on the political spectrum. Materials in each chapter include opinions in which authors clearly disagree as well as alternative opinions in which authors may agree on a broader issue but disagree on the possible solutions. In this way, the content of each volume in Current Controversies mirrors the mosaic of opinions encountered in society. Readers will quickly realize that there are many viable answers to these complex issues. By questioning each author's conclusions, students and casual readers can begin to develop the critical thinking skills so important to evaluating opinionated material.

Current Controversies is also ideal for controlled research. Each anthology in the series is composed of primary sources taken from a wide gamut of informational categories including periodicals, newspapers, books, US and foreign government documents, and the publications of private and public organizations. Readers will find factual support for reports, debates, and research papers covering all areas of important issues. In addition, an annotated table of contents, an index, a book and periodical bibliography, and a list of organizations to contact are included in each book to expedite further research.

Perhaps more than ever before in history, people are confronted with diverse and contradictory information. During the Persian Gulf War, for example, the public was not only treated to minute-to-minute coverage of the war, it was also inundated with critiques of the coverage and countless analyses of the factors motivating US involvement. Being able to sort through the plethora of opinions accompanying today's major issues, and to draw one's own conclusions, can be a complicated and frustrating struggle. It is the editors' hope that Current Controversies will help readers with this struggle.

Introduction

"Even once the issue of state law has been decided, there are a host of other issues involving the regulation of medical marijuana that create controversy."

The issue of medical marijuana, or cannabis, has become widely debated in recent years, as numerous states have legalized the use of cannabis for qualified patients. As of September 2010, fourteen states and the District of Columbia have enacted laws that allow the use of medical marijuana, and several other states continue to consider the issue. California was the first state to implement a law legalizing marijuana for medical use, and a look at the history of medical marijuana in California illustrates some of the issues, challenges, and debates about the use of marijuana as medicine.

California Proposition 215, also known as the Compassionate Use Act of 1996, was put forth to California voters on November 5, 1996. The proposition called for the removal of state-level criminal penalties on the use, possession, and cultivation of marijuana by patients, where such use "has been recommended by a physician who has determined that the person's health would benefit from the use of marijuana." Debate over the proposition was fierce. Within the ballot literature, doctors Richard J. Cohen and Ivan Silverberg and registered nurse Anna T. Boyce argued, "Today, physicians are allowed to prescribe powerful drugs like morphine and codeine. It doesn't make sense that they cannot prescribe marijuana, too." But opponents of the proposition James P. Fox, Dr. Michael J. Meyers, and Sharon Rose argued, "The proponents of this deceptive and poorly written initiative want to exploit public compassion for the sick in order to legalize and legitimatize the widespread use of marijuana in California." Proposition 215 passed with just over 55 percent of voters approving it.

Concerned about the lack of guidelines on medical marijuana use within the proposition, the California legislature passed Senate Bill 420, effective January 1, 2004, which put into place guidelines for the legal use of medical marijuana in California. Among other regulations, the bill created a voluntary identification card program for qualified medical marijuana users "in order to avoid unnecessary arrest and prosecution of these individuals and provide needed guidance to law enforcement officers." The bill also placed a limit on possession, limiting marijuana possession to "eight ounces of dried marijuana per qualified patient" and "no more than six mature or 12 immature marijuana plants per qualified patient," unless a doctor or local authority allows otherwise. In addition, the bill allowed for patients to "cultivate marijuana for medical purposes" through nonprofit collectives or cooperatives, though such marijuana transactions are subject to sales tax.

One of the ongoing contentious issues regarding California's medical marijuana policy is the existence of medical marijuana dispensaries. In a 2009 white paper, the California Police Chiefs Association claimed, "Marijuana dispensaries are commonly large moneymaking enterprises that will sell marijuana to most anyone who produces a physician's written recommendation for its medical use." The association expressed concern that the dispensaries "have been tied to organized criminal gangs, foster large grow operations, and are often multimillion-dollar profit centers." As noted by Attorney General Edmund G. Brown Jr. in his August 2008 publication "Guidelines for the Security and Non-Diversion of Marijuana Grown for Medical Use," dispensaries must act as cooperatives or collectives under the law. Brown notes, "Dispensaries that merely require patients to complete a form summarily designating the business owner as their primary caregiver—and then offering marijuana in exchange for cash 'donations'—are likely unlawful."

One place where the battle about medical marijuana dispensaries is being played out is in Los Angeles. From 2007 to 2009, the number of medical marijuana dispensaries had grown to more than eight hundred in Los Angeles and there were many complaints about their widespread existence. The Los Angeles City Council approved an ordinance in January 2010 to cap the number of permitted dispensaries within the city at seventy and placed restrictions on where the dispensaries may be located. In April the city began cracking down on dispensaries that were not legally registered, and the number of dispensaries started dropping. Some medical marijuana patients have expressed concern about the closing of dispensaries. This issue will continue to be played out, as a series of lawsuits and countersuits over city regulations still need to be decided in court.

Another issue faced by California and other states that have removed state restrictions on the medical use of marijuana is the fact that such state legislation does not undo federal legislation restricting the use of marijuana. The 1970 Controlled Substances Act (CSA) established a federal regulatory system designed to combat recreational drug abuse by making it unlawful to manufacture, distribute, dispense, or possess marijuana and other drugs. As Attorney General Brown notes in his 2008 guidelines, "California did not 'legalize' medical marijuana, but instead exercised the state's reserved powers to not punish certain marijuana offenses under state law when a physician has recommended its use to treat a serious medical condition." The tension between state laws and federal law continues to cause confusion and debate about whether states have the power to legalize medical marijuana and whether the federal government should intervene.

The use of medical marijuana will continue to have vocal proponents and opponents. And, as California illustrates, even once the issue of state law has been decided, there are a host of other issues involving the regulation of medical marijuana that create controversy. The issues of whether marijuana should be a medical option and the ways in which marijuana use should be regulated by the government are just a few of the fascinating debates about the medical use of cannabis explored in *Current Controversies: Medical Marijuana*.

CHAPTER 1

Should Marijuana Be a Medical Option?

Overview: The Debate About Marijuana as a Medicine

Anna Wilde Mathews

Anna Wilde Mathews writes the weekly Healthy Consumer column in the Wall Street Journal, *focusing on health insurance and the financial aspects of health care.*

Charlene DeGidio never smoked marijuana in the 1960s, or afterward. But a year ago [2009], after medications failed to relieve the pain in her legs and feet, a doctor suggested that the Adna, Wash., retiree try the drug.

Patient Access to Medical Marijuana

Ms. DeGidio, 69 years old, bought candy with marijuana mixed in. It worked in easing her neuropathic pain, for which doctors haven't been able to pinpoint a cause, she says. Now, Ms. DeGidio, who had previously tried without success other drugs including Neurontin and lidocaine patches, nibbles marijuana-laced peppermint bars before sleep, and keeps a bag in her refrigerator that she's warned her grandchildren to avoid.

"It's not like you're out smoking pot for enjoyment or to get high," says the former social worker, who won't take the drug during the day because she doesn't want to feel disoriented. "It's a medicine."

For many patients like Ms. DeGidio, it's getting easier to access marijuana for medical use. The U.S. Department of Justice has said it will not generally prosecute ill people under doctors' care whose use of the drug complies with state rules. New Jersey will become the 14th state to allow therapeutic use of marijuana, and the number is likely to grow. Illinois and New York, among others, are considering new laws.

Anna Wilde Mathews, "Is Marijuana a Medicine?" *Wall Street Journal*, January 18, 2010. Reproduced by permission.

The Studies on Medical Marijuana

As the legal landscape for patients clears somewhat, the medical one remains confusing, largely because of limited scientific studies. A recent American Medical Association [AMA] review found fewer than 20 randomized, controlled clinical trials of smoked marijuana for all possible uses. These involved around 300 people in all—well short of the evidence typically required for a pharmaceutical to be marketed in the U.S.

Doctors say the studies that have been done suggest marijuana can benefit patients in the areas of managing neuropathic pain, which is caused by certain types of nerve injury, and in bolstering appetite and treating nausea, for instance in cancer patients undergoing chemotherapy. "The evidence is mounting" for those uses, says Igor Grant, director of the Center for Medicinal Cannabis Research at the University of California, San Diego.

But in a range of other conditions for which marijuana has been considered, such as epilepsy and immune diseases like lupus, there's scant and inconclusive research to show the drug's effectiveness. Marijuana also has been tied to side effects including a racing heart and short-term memory loss and, in at least a few cases, anxiety and psychotic experiences such as hallucinations. The Food and Drug Administration doesn't regulate marijuana, so the quality and potency of the product available in medical-marijuana dispensaries can vary.

The Controversy About Medical Marijuana

Though states have been legalizing medical use of marijuana since 1996, when California passed a ballot initiative, the idea remains controversial. Opponents say such laws can open a door to wider cultivation and use of the drug by people without serious medical conditions. That concern is heightened, they say, when broadly written statutes, such as California's, allow wide leeway for doctors to decide when to write marijuana recommendations.

But advocates of medical-marijuana laws say certain seriously ill patients can benefit from the drug and should be able to access it with a doctor's permission. They argue that some patients may get better results from marijuana than from available prescription drugs.

The relatively limited research supporting medical marijuana poses practical challenges for doctors and patients who want to consider it as a therapeutic option.

Glenn Osaki, 51, a technology consultant from Pleasanton, Calif., says he smokes marijuana to counter nausea and pain. Diagnosed in 2005 with advanced colon cancer, he has had his entire colon removed, creating digestive problems, and suffers neuropathic pain in his hands and feet from a chemotherapy drug. He says smoking marijuana was more effective and faster than prescription drugs he tried, including one that is a synthetic version of marijuana's most active ingredient, known as THC [tetrahydrocannabinol].

Challenges for Doctors, Patients, and Researchers

The relatively limited research supporting medical marijuana poses practical challenges for doctors and patients who want to consider it as a therapeutic option. It's often unclear when, or whether, it might work better than traditional drugs for particular people. Unlike prescription drugs it comes with no established dosing regimen.

"I don't know what to recommend to patients about what to use, how much to use, where to get it," says Scott Fishman, chief of pain medicine at the University of California, Davis medical school, who says he rarely writes marijuana recommendations, typically only at a patient's request.

Researchers say it's difficult to get funding and federal approval for marijuana research. In November, the AMA urged the federal government to review marijuana's position in the most-restricted category of drugs, so it could be studied more easily.

Gregory T. Carter, a University of Washington professor of rehabilitation medicine, says he's developed his own procedures for recommending marijuana, which he does for some patients with serious neuromuscular conditions such as amyotrophic lateral sclerosis, or Lou Gehrig's disease, to treat pain and other symptoms. He typically urges those who haven't tried it before to start with a few puffs using a vaporizer, which heats the marijuana to release its active chemicals, then wait 10 minutes. He warns them to have family nearby and to avoid driving, and he checks back with them after a few days. Many are "surprised at how mild" the drug's psychotropic effects are, he says.

States' rules on growing and dispensing medical marijuana vary. Some states license specialized dispensaries. These can range from small storefronts to bigger operations that feel more like pharmacies. Typically, they have security procedures to limit walk-in visitors.

At least a few dispensaries say they inspect their suppliers and use labs to check the potency of their product, though states don't generally require such measures. "It's difficult to understand how we can call it medicine if we don't know what's in it," says Stephen DeAngelo, executive director of the Harborside Health Center, a medical-marijuana dispensary in Oakland, Calif.

Possible Benefits of Medical Marijuana

Some of the strongest research results support the idea of using marijuana to relieve neuropathic pain. For example, a trial of 50 AIDS patients published in the journal *Neurology* in 2007 found that 52% of those who smoked marijuana reported a 30% or greater reduction in pain. Just 24% of those who got placebo cigarettes reported the same lessening of pain.

Marijuana has also been shown to affect nausea and appetite. The AMA review said three controlled studies with 43 total participants showed a "modest" antinausea effect of smoked marijuana in cancer patients undergoing chemotherapy. Studies of HIV-positive patients have suggested that smoked marijuana can improve appetite and trigger weight gain.

Donald Abrams, a doctor and professor at the University of California, San Francisco who has studied marijuana, says he recommends it to some cancer patients, including those who haven't found standard antinausea drugs effective and some with loss of appetite.

Possible Risks of Medical Marijuana

Side effects can be a problem for some people. Thea Sagen, 62, an advanced neuroendocrine cancer patient in Seaside, Calif., says she expected something like a pharmacy when she went to a marijuana dispensary mentioned by her oncologist. She says she was disappointed to find that the staffers couldn't say which of the products, with names like Pot o' Gold and Blockbuster, might boost her flagging appetite or soothe her anxiety. "They said, 'it's trial and error,'" she says. "I was in there flying blind, looking at all this stuff."

Ms. Sagen says she bought several items and tried one-eighth teaspoon of marijuana-infused honey. After a few hours, she was hallucinating, too dizzy and confused to dress herself for a doctor's appointment. Then came vomiting far worse than her stomach upset before she took the drug. When she reported the side effects to her oncologist's nurse and her primary care physician, she got no guidance. She doesn't take the drug now. But with advice from a nutritionist, her appetite and food intake have improved, she says.

Other marijuana users may experience the well-known reduction in ability to concentrate. At least a few users suffer troubling short-term psychiatric side effects, which can include anxiety and panic. More controversially, an analysis published in the journal *Lancet* in 2007 tied marijuana use to a higher rate of psychotic conditions such as schizophrenia. But the analysis noted that such a link doesn't necessarily show marijuana is a cause of the conditions.

Long-term marijuana use can lead to physical dependence, though it is not as addictive as nicotine or alcohol, says Margaret Haney, a professor at Columbia University's medical school. Smoked marijuana may also risk lung irritation, but a large 2006 study, published in *Cancer Epidemiology, Biomarkers & Prevention*, found no tie to lung cancer.

Marijuana Has Been Proven to Effectively Treat Many Medical Conditions

David Bearman

David Bearman is a physician in California who specializes in pain management and cannabinoid medicine.

We stand at the dawn of a new era for medicinal cannabis [marijuana]. Since 1964, when Dr. Raphael Mechoulam, of [the Hebrew University of] Jerusalem, isolated tetrahydrocannabinol (THC) [the main psychoactive substance in marijuana] we have learned more about the marvels of the brain's neurochemistry. There has developed a greater understanding of the role of serotonin in depression and we have had the discovery of endorphins, the naturally occurring opiates, and the endocannabinoid system. In 1992, Professor Mechoulam described the endocannabinoid system. He characterized the endogenous cannabinoid receptors and the endogenous cannabinoids that bind to these receptors.

We have crossed the threshold into exciting cannabis-related treatments for many conditions and symptoms. Cannabis gives relief from chronic pain which arises from a myriad of pain-producing illnesses; cannabis provides both analgesia and anti-inflammatory relief for autoimmune diseases such as rheumatoid arthritis, fibromyalgia, complex sympathetic dystrophy, and restless leg syndrome; and assists many with mental health problems, including attention deficit disorder (ADD), post-traumatic stress disorder (PTSD), depression, and obsessive compulsive disorder (OCD)—to name but a few conditions which have been shown to benefit from cannabis and cannabinoids. . . .

David Bearman, "Medical Marijuana: Scientific Mechanisms and Clinical Indications," www.davidbearmanmd.com, n.d. pp. 1, 4–14, 17–18. Reproduced by permission.

Marijuana in the US Pharmacopeia

Cannabis was in the United States Pharmacopeia (USP) [the nongovernmental, official public standards-setting authority for prescription and over-the-counter medicines] from 1854 until 1941. During that time it was the third or fourth most common ingredient in patent medicines. Prominent drug companies, such as Squibb, Eli Lilly, Merck, and Parke-Davis all had products that contained cannabis. People consumed these medicants with benefit and without reporting significant adverse side effects.

In the 1920s and 1930s, as medicine evolved into the modern medicine of today, manufactured pharmaceuticals began to appear. The increasing numbers and presumed specificity of these manufactured pharmaceuticals caused many to discount herbal medicine. Many of the modern physicians of the 30s, 40s and 50s did not believe that plants which grew naturally and were used by primitives could be as effective as manufactured pharmaceuticals produced by chemists and pharmacologists.

Federal control in the United States over medicinal cannabis began in the late 1930s. First came the 1937 Marihuana Tax Act. This law did not make cannabis illegal. Instead it added bureaucratic impediments which made it more cumbersome for drug companies to use cannabis in medications. It became necessary for pharmaceutical companies to keep records on cannabis and to pay a tax on its use. Therefore many drug companies began to omit cannabis from their medications.

Then, the Federal Food, Drug, and Cosmetic Act (1938) came about. It was passed as a result of a sulfa drug produced by Massengill that sadly contained a compound similar to antifreeze. This led to the death of 100 people. It was this act that gave the Food and Drug Administration (FDA) the power to decide whether or not a drug was safe. As a result of this, all future pharmaceuticals required the FDA to certify their safety.

This 1938 law grandfathered in the medications, including cannabis, that were on the market at that time. Soon in 1942, cannabis fell out of the United States Pharmacopeia. This was largely because drug companies were not using it anymore. Later cannabis was bureaucratically and arbitrarily categorized as a "new" drug and therefore was required to be covered by the 1938 act. A legal challenge is currently in the courts that cannabis does not require FDA approval because it is covered by the grandfather clause.

The Government Response to Medical Marijuana Research

In 1969, the Marihuana Tax Act was declared unconstitutional in a case involving famed 60's guru and former Harvard professor, Timothy Leary, Ph.D., whose mantra was "Turn on, tune in, drop out." However, we are now constrained by the Controlled Substances Act, which was passed in 1970. Cannabis is placed in Schedule I, which is reserved for drugs which have no known medical use in the US. This law is thought by many conservative Republicans to abuse the 9th and 10th amendments to the Constitution, which limit the powers of the federal government and protect state's rights.

The United States government has largely stood in the way of constructive research regarding the medicinal use of cannabis.

Between 1978 and 1992, a program called the Compassionate Investigational New Drug (IND) program, existed in the US. The purpose of this government program was to provide cannabis to patients who the government deemed received medicinal value from it. It required going through a cumbersome bureaucracy to get approval. At its height the IND had 15 patients enrolled in the program and 25 more approved (some texts say the numbers were 12 on the program and 28 or 35 approved). Each one on the program, be it 12 or 15, received 300 hand-rolled 0.9 gram cannabis cigarettes per month from the federal government.

The program was closed to new entrants in 1991 because too many people were applying. In the words of Dr. [James O.] Mason, head of the United States Public Health Service at the time, the first Bush administration was concerned that if too many patients were on the program, the public might get the idea that marijuana was actually good for you. In fact if hundreds of patients were on the program it would have made it difficult for the federal government to continue to contend that marijuana has no medical value. There are still five surviving patients who remain in the program, four who receive their 300 marijuana cigarettes each month in the mail; the fifth gets his 300 every three (3) weeks.

The United States government has largely stood in the way of constructive research regarding the medicinal use of cannabis. One of the leading medicinal cannabis practitioners in California, and in the United States, was the late Dr. Tod Mikuriya, who was in charge of marijuana research for the federal government at the National Institute of Mental Health (NIMH) for a short period of time in the late 1960s. Mikuriya was very familiar with the "Indian Hemp [Drugs] Commission Report" (1894), produced by the British in India, having read all 3340 pages of it. He was very excited about scientifically exploring the possibilities surrounding the medicinal use of cannabis. However, Mikuriya soon found that the government was more excited about finding out about anything that was wrong with cannabis. The government made clear their aversion to understanding how cannabis worked and why it had been used medicinally for at least 3000 years. So NIMH and Mikuriya soon parted company.

Current federal drug czar John Walters [director of the Office of National Drug Control Policy (ONDCP) from 2001 to 2009], has said that there is no research that shows that cannabis is useful from a medicinal point of view. Former drug czar General [Barry] McCaffrey has said that cannabis was Cheech and Chong [referring to the comedy duo consisting of Richard "Cheech" Marin and Tommy Chong] medicine. Both of these bureaucrats have evidently done limited literature searches into the subject. If they had, they would have found that there has been quite a lot of research into the medicinal use of cannabis both here and abroad. Much of this research has produced positive findings about cannabis's medicinal efficacy.

20th-Century Medical Marijuana Research

The first modern study of the medicinal use of cannabis was conducted in 1949. The results of that study suggested that cannabis may be useful in dealing with seizures. Not surprisingly, I have a number of patients today, who get a great deal of relief from seizures by using cannabis. In the 1970s and 1980s studies were conducted in eight different states, including Georgia, Tennessee, New York, California, and New Mexico, which demonstrated that cannabis was useful in treating nausea and as an appetite stimulant.

The next breakthrough for the modern-day medicinal use of cannabis occurred in 1985. In response to increasing medicinal use of cannabis by AIDS patients and cancer victims, the US government encouraged the development and approval of synthetic delta-9-THC. This product is marketed under the trade name Marinol. It does have therapeutic benefits. The FDA has approved it for treatment of nausea in cancer patients and/or treatment for appetite stimulation in AIDS patients. Off label, it has been used to treat pain, ADD and other conditions. I am the largest prescriber of Marinol in the Santa Barbara County. However, I find that it has more side effects, costs more, and does not work as well as cannabis and may cause dysphoria. Nevertheless for many, it is effective with few side effects.

In 1992, Mechoulam characterized the endocannabinoid system, the system of receptor sites and neurotransmitters that explains why cannabis affects us as it does. Even though we know less about the enocannabinoid system than other neurotransmitter system, the endocannabinoid system is the largest neurotransmitter system in the brain.

Another great leap forward in the modern-day medicinal cannabis research came about in 1999, when GW Pharmaceuticals, a British phytochemical company, started to conduct research on six different strains of cannabis and combinations of these strains. They developed different tinctures of cannabis delivered under the tongue via a metered sprayer.

GW's research effort was in response to the 1997 report of the House of Lord's Science and Technology Committee and a growing need to address the medical needs of British multiple sclerosis (MS) patients who were being arrested for possession of marijuana in embarrassing numbers. The MS patients were using marijuana because it was providing relief from muscle spasm and pain with few side effects.

Cannabis is of great benefit to a vast number of people with a wide range of conditions.

21st-Century Medical Marijuana Research

In 2000, the [Center for Medicinal Cannabis] Research (CMCR) was set up at the University of California [UC] at San Diego School of Medicine. The CMCR has administered more than eighteen FDA-approved smoked cannabis medical studies done at four UC medical schools, including a study by Dr. Daniel Abrams *et al* published in the February 2007 issue of the *Journal of Neurology*. Abrams's study was designed to determine the effect of smoked cannabis on the neuropathic pain of HIV-associated sensory neuropathy. The results showed that even the government's low-grade cannabis was capable of reducing daily pain by 34%. These results led the authors to conclude: "Smoked cannabis was well tolerated and effectively relieved chronic neuropathic pain from HIV-associated sensory neuropathy. The findings are comparable to oral drugs used for chronic neuropathic pain."

Research conducted by Dr. Donald Tashkin, a noted pulmonologist at UCLA [University of California, Los Angeles], has found revealing and possible counterintuitive findings about the pulmonary effects of cannabis. Some of Tashkin's research clearly shows that cannabis is a bronchodilator and is useful in treating asthma. This is consistent with the historical fact that in the 1920s Australia and France had cannabis-containing smokables for treatment of asthma.

Another of Tashkin's studies, reported at the 2006 International Cannabinoid Research Society (ICRS), demonstrated that cannabis smokers actually have a reduced risk of lung cancer over nonsmokers. Tashkin states that more research is needed to confirm or refute this finding. But when paired with the Kaiser Permanente survey of 65,000 patient charts which found no difference in cancers of the mouth, throat and lungs in people who smoked nothing and those who smoked cannabis, it strongly suggests that smoking cannabis either lowers cancers of the respiratory tree or has no effect on respiratory cancer rates. . . .

Conditions That May Be Treated with Marijuana

Cannabis is of great benefit to a vast number of people with a wide range of conditions. Tens of millions more would benefit if it were obtainable through conventional distribution. Pain is the number one condition treated with cannabis by doctors in California, Oregon, and Colorado—three of the 12 states in which it is legal to use cannabis under state law if it is approved or recommended by a physician. Migraine is another condition for which cannabis can be extremely effective. Some of my patients have told me that if they take cannabis with the onset of their migraine prodrome it prevents the migraine from developing. Other migraine sufferers say that while cannabis does not prevent the migraine from occurring, it makes them less severe and does help to control the symptoms.

Cannabis can also provide great relief from nausea, is an appetite stimulant, and helps with depression. All of which are of great benefit to AIDS and cancer patients. Cannabis seems to be particularly good at dealing with pain issues associated with arthritic or autoimmune conditions. This is likely because of its analgesic and anti-inflammatory properties. Of course, it is well known that cannabis is useful for helping people with sleeping difficulties.

Many leading figures and organizations have publicly supported the medicinal cannabis movement.

Other conditions that cannabis may benefit include: seizures, glaucoma—cannabis decreases intraocular pressure by approximately 25%—peripheral neuropathy, asthma, and irritable bowel syndrome [IBS]. Research by Professor Daniele Piomelli, a pharmacologist at the University of California, Irvine, demonstrates that cannabis may also be of benefit to people with bipolar disorder, Tourette's syndrome, ADD, and panic attacks. Clinical experience supports Professor Piomelli's contention.

One of the most exciting uses for cannabis is for treatment of PTSD. This is very important for servicemen returning from the war in Iraq. In California, unlike other states where the medicinal use of cannabis is legal, we do not only have a discrete list of conditions that physicians are allowed to recommend cannabis for. California has a list of specific conditions, but physicians also have the legal right to use their discretion to recommend cannabis for "any other medical condition" for which we feel cannabis will be medically useful. This has allowed cannabis use for the psychological problems noted above.

Support for the Medical Marijuana Movement

The medical marijuana movement has had its fair share of critics. The majority of them do not have a medical background. The critics tend to be of the belief that the medicinal use of cannabis is a hoax, and has more to do with legalizing cannabis for recreational purposes than to relieve the symptoms of people who are ill. If something (say Valium or morphine) has medicinal value and people want to utilize it therapeutically, that does not mean that society is also sanctioning its recreational use. These are two different issues and this effort to confuse the two is unfortunate because cannabis has significant medicinal value.

Fortunately, many leading figures and organizations have publicly supported the medicinal cannabis movement. The former surgeon general of the United States, Dr. Joycelyn Elders, said that there is an overwhelming amount of evidence to show that cannabis can relieve certain types of pain. [The authors of] a 1997 editorial published in the *New England Journal of Medicine* said that they thought that the federal policy of preventing physicians from prescribing marijuana for ill patients was "misguided, heavy-handed, and inhumane." Furthermore, the government-funded Institute of Medicine report into the medicinal use of marijuana concluded that cannabis does indeed have medicinal properties.

Dr. Andrea Barthwell, who served as deputy director for demand reduction in the Office of National Drug Control Policy (ONDCP) between 2002 and 2005, has had an interesting changing of position. During her time at the ONDCP she was highly critical of medical marijuana. However, she is now a paid lobbyist for GW Pharmaceuticals, the company that makes Sativex, which is the tincture of cannabis.

Another person who seems to have dramatically changed his opinion on medical marijuana is Bob Barr, a former member of the United States House of Representatives. Barr was a vigorous opponent of marijuana and a strong supporter of the War on Drugs. However, since joining the Libertarian Party, Barr has seemingly reversed his previous opinions. He is now a paid lobbyist for the Marijuana Policy Project, whose goal is to legalize the recreational use of marijuana. He bases this change on solid Libertarian philosophy—that after 9/11 [September 11, 2001, terrorist attacks on the United States] the federal government accrued too much power to itself at the expense of the states. . . .

Marijuana's Medicinal Effects

Cannabis is a 21-carbon molecule that contains 483 chemicals, of which 66 are cannabinoids. Many of the 483 compounds have medicinal value. Research continues to gain more knowledge about these molecules. Recently a hearing was held before the DEA [Drug Enforcement Administration] chief administrative law judge Mary Ellen Bittner. The DEA was ordered to give a license to Dr. Albert Craker at the University of Massachusetts, who is an expert in medicinal plants, so that he could grow cannabis. His research goal is investigation of the ingredients in various strains of cannabis to determine which of the chemicals are most effective at treating the wide variety of medical conditions that respond to the medicinal use of cannabis.

How does cannabis exert its medicinal effects? The medicinal effects of cannabis are mediated by the endocannabinoid system. An increase in cannabinoids either endogenous [within] or exogenous [outside], increases the amount of the neurotransmitter dopamine in the brain. We know that dopamine acts in a different way to any other neurotransmitter. Instead of stimulating the next neuron on the pathway up the CNS [central nervous system], dopamine actually doubles back on itself and depolarizes the neuron that just released it by reversing the concentration of sodium and potassium inside and outside the cell. The effect of this is that it slows down neurotransmission.

Cannabis has provided millions worldwide with relief from chronic pain caused by a myriad of pain-producing illnesses.

So, if a person is having migraines caused by an overload of the electrical circuits in a certain part of the brain, slowing down the speed of neurotransmission leads to fewer neural impulses, which in turn, decreases the likelihood or severity of a migraine. The same thing is true of people that have panic attacks. If you have negative thoughts that are moving at warp speed to the midbrain, you are overwhelming the emotional control center of the brain, the limbic system. Cannabis slows down the speed of neurotransmission, exposing the cerebral cortex to fewer slower-moving neural stimuli. This allows the higher centers of the brain to have time to more rationally assess the relative danger or the negativity and put a more rational point of view on that sensory input.

One suggestion is that cannabis and cannabinoids increase the amount of free dopamine in the brain by freeing dopamine from binding to another neurochemical, dopamine transporter. The dopamine transporter and dopamine bond form an electrochemical bond. This ties up the dopamine so the dopamine is not free to act as one of the brain's "off switches." We were all taught in medical school that 70% of the brain is there to turn off the other 30%—dopamine is one of the "off switches" that helps modulate sensory input. Therefore, if there is not enough dopamine present in the brain, certain parts of it become overloaded, and the illness you have depends upon the part or parts of the midbrain that is being overloaded.

Cannabinoids compete with dopamine for the binding sites on the dopamine transporter, and in sufficient quantity it wins, thus freeing up more dopamine to help slow down the speed of neurotransmissions. This, in my opinion and many others, is responsible for much of the therapeutic value of cannabis. Although it has effects on certain receptor sites in the brain that contribute to its therapeutic value, it probably directly affects the appetite and sleep centers in the brain, decreases the perception of pain and centrally decreases nausea. Peripherally cannabinoids stimulate CB2 [cannabinoid] receptors in the GI [gastrointestinal] tract which is what makes cannabis valuable in treating Crohn's disease and IBS. . . .

The Current Issue

Where do we go from here? The question is whether or not we are going to let people take responsibility for their own health. Why should people suffer unnecessarily? Cannabis has provided millions worldwide with relief from chronic pain caused by a myriad of pain-producing illnesses. Cannabis has significantly improved the quality of life of people with cancer, AIDS, arthritis, and the list goes on. The medical marijuana movement is not concerned with decriminalizing or legalizing cannabis for recreational use. It is concerned with helping people with serious illnesses and disabilities to get on with their lives.

The issue is will the pharmaceutical companies take control over the medical use of this plant through patenting strains and creating synthetic cannabinoids while being protected by the government, or will people be able to grow a safe, cheap, effective medication.

Studies Show Marijuana Can Be an Effective Medicine for Pain

Center for Medicinal Cannabis Research

The Center for Medicinal Cannabis Research conducts scientific studies intended to determine the general medical safety and efficacy of marijuana products.

Chronic pain—pain on a daily or almost daily basis for six months or longer—is one of the most prevalent and disabling conditions in California and in the US generally. Whereas many types of pain are caused by stimulation of specialized pain receptors on nerve endings due to injury of tissues, neuropathic pain is produced either by direct damage to the central (brain, spinal cord) or peripheral nervous system itself, or by abnormal functioning of these systems. Infections, diabetes, physical trauma, strokes, and many other diseases can injure the nervous system, with resulting pain, which persists even though pain receptors themselves are not directly activated. It is therefore not surprising that neuropathic pain is widespread, affecting 5–10% of the US population. Only a few classes of medications are approved for use as analgesics in these conditions (opioids, anticonvulsants, antidepressants), and many patients obtain only partial relief, even when using combinations of all available therapies. Among the most difficult to treat neuropathic pain conditions are those secondary to HIV, diabetes, and to physical trauma to the nervous system. Because these neuropathic disorders are so prevalent, and treatment alternatives are so limited, the CMCR [Center for Medical Cannabis Research] focused on these conditions.

Center for Medicinal Cannabis Research, "Report to the Legislature and Governor of the State of California Presenting Findings Pursuant to SB847 Which Created the CMCR and Provided State Funding," University of California, February 11, 2010, pp. 8–12, 16. Courtesy of the Center for Medicinal Cannabis Research.

Research on Marijuana for Pain

A distinguishing scientific feature of the program of pain research, made possible only by the coordinating function of the CMCR, is the commonality of measures and methods across the research studies. This allows for the distinctive advantage of comparability of results across studies. Additionally, when possible we studied treatment of the same type of pain condition (e.g., HIV neuropathy) in more than one geographic site. Finding comparable results at two or more sites studying the same disease is scientifically important, since this suggests that the results are generally valid, rather than being due to chance or the specific characteristics of a single sample of patients, or of a particular team of researchers.

This research used the gold standard design for assessment of therapeutic effects, the randomized clinical trial. In this approach participants are assigned by chance, like flipping a coin, to an experimental treatment, in this case cannabis, or to a placebo (an inactive treatment). The placebo in all of our studies was a marijuana (cannabis) cigarette, made with cannabis from which the "active" ingredients, for example delta-9-tetrahydrocannabinol (THC), had been removed. The cigarette therefore had the appearance and the aroma of a marijuana cigarette, but without the crucial chemical ingredients hypothesized to be therapeutically active. Randomization ensures factors which might skew the results (like age, duration or intensity of pain) are equally present in both the experimental and placebo condition. Placebo is essential, since the expectation of pain relief from any treatment is a powerful analgesic itself. All of our protocols used measures of pain recommended by expert consensus as standard in the field. For studies of smoked cannabis, the researchers used a standard, timed method of inhalation; research using vaporized cannabis used similar, state-of-the art technology. Researchers measured blood concentrations of the primary active ingredient of cannabis (THC), allowing estimates of relationships between dose, concentration, and magnitude of pain relief.

Results of Recent Studies

To date, the CMCR has completed four studies in the treatment of neuropathic pain. Two studies have focused on neuropathic pain resulting from HIV infection or the drugs used to treat HIV, one has focused on neuropathic pain of varying causes, and one has used an experimental model of neuropathic pain tested in healthy volunteers. The results from these four studies have been convergent, with all four demonstrating a significant decrease in pain after cannabis administration. The magnitude of effect in these studies, expressed as the number of patients needed to treat to produce one positive outcome, was comparable to current therapies. Two additional studies involving neuropathic pain are under way.

Multiple sclerosis (MS) is one of the most common chronic and disabling diseases of the nervous system. Caused by loss of the insulating sheath surrounding nerve fibers, the disease usually begins in young adulthood. Although it may initially wax and wane in intensity and be of mild severity, it often steadily progresses, causing fatigue, loss of balance, muscle weakness, and muscle spasticity. Affecting up to 70% of people with the disease, muscle spasms lead to pain, inability to walk, and difficulties with self-care, causing most of the everyday life disability from this disease. There is as yet no cure for MS. Treatments for muscle spasticity are only partially effective and have side effects which are not easily tolerated, making the search for new therapies of high importance. Given this background, the CMCR identified MS spasticity as an additional target for therapeutic research. As with all CMCR studies, the research used the most rigorous scientific approach to testing therapies, a randomized clinical trial, supplemented by modern measurement of muscle spasticity, everyday function, life quality, and side effects. Results to date have found a significant improvement in both an objective measure of spasticity and pain intensity in patients whose standard therapy had provided inadequate relief.

Medical Marijuana for HIV-Related Neuropathic Pain

The primary objective of this study ["The Effect of Cannabis on Neuropathic Pain in HIV-Related Peripheral Neuropathy"] was to evaluate the efficacy of smoked cannabis when used as an analgesic in persons with neuropathic pain from HIV-associated distal sensory polyneuropathy (DSPN). In a double-blind, randomized, five-day clinical trial patients received either smoked cannabis or placebo cannabis cigarettes. Patients continued on any concurrent analgesic medications (e.g., gabapentin, amitriptyline, narcotics, NSAIDs [nonsteroidal anti-inflammatory drugs]) which they were prescribed prior to the trial; the dose and amount of the medications were recorded daily.

The full results of this study appear in the journal *Neurology*. In brief, 55 patients were randomized and 50 completed the entire trial. Smoked cannabis reduced daily pain by 34% compared to 17% with placebo. The study concluded that a significantly greater proportion of patients who smoked cannabis (52%) had a greater than 30% reduction in pain intensity compared to only 24% in the placebo group. This result is clinically important, since the threshold of a 30% reduction in pain intensity is associated with meaningful improvement in quality of life in other research on pain outcomes.

Cannabis appeared to be well tolerated and there were no safety concerns raised. By design, all patients had smoking experience with cannabis. There were more side effects in those receiving cannabis than placebo, with the most frequent being sedation, anxiety, and dizziness, but these were all rated as "mild."

Medical Marijuana for Painful HIV Neuropathy

The primary objective of this study ["Placebo-Controlled, Double Blind Trial of Medicinal Cannabis in Painful HIV Neuropathy"] also was to evaluate the efficacy of smoked cannabis when used as an analgesic in persons with HIV-associated painful neuropathy. In a double-blind, randomized, clinical trial of the short-term adjunctive treatment of neuropathic pain in HIV-associated distal sensory polyneuropathy, participants received either smoked cannabis or placebo cannabis cigarettes. A structured dose escalation-titration protocol was used to find an individualized, effective, safe, and well-tolerated dose for each subject. Participants continued on their usual analgesic medications throughout the trial, with the dose and amount of these medications being recorded daily.

> *Both low and high cannabis doses were efficacious in reducing neuropathic pain of diverse causes.*

The full results of this study were published in the journal *Neuropsychopharmacology*. In brief, 34 eligible subjects enrolled and 28 completed both cannabis and placebo treatments. Among completers, pain relief was significantly greater with cannabis than placebo. The proportion of subjects achieving at least 30% pain relief was again significantly greater with cannabis (46%) compared to placebo (18%). It was concluded that smoked cannabis was generally well tolerated and effective when added to concomitant analgesic therapy in patients with medically refractory pain due to HIV-associated neuropathy. Once again these results appeared to be relevant to everyday clinical practice, because the magnitude of pain relief is associated with that which improves life quality, and also because the benefit was above and beyond that conferred by the patients' usual analgesics.

As in the study described above, side effects were more frequent with cannabis than with placebo, with the most common being sleepiness or sedation, fatigue, and difficulty with concentration. These were "mild" for the most part and did not raise safety concerns.

Medical Marijuana for a Variety of Neuropathic Pain

This study's objective ["A Double-Blind, Placebo-Controlled Crossover Trial of the Antinociceptive Effects of Smoked Marijuana on Subjects with Neuropathic Pain"] was to examine the efficacy of two doses of smoked cannabis on pain in persons with neuropathic pain of different origins (e.g., physical trauma to nerve bundles, spinal cord injury, multiple sclerosis, diabetes). In a double-blind, randomized clinical trial participants received either low-dose, high-dose, or placebo cannabis cigarettes. As customary in CMCR trials, participants were allowed to continue their usual regimen of pain medications (e.g., codeine, morphine, and others).

The full results of this study have been published in the *Journal of Pain*. Thirty-eight patients underwent a standardized procedure for smoking either high-dose (7%), low-dose (3.5%), or placebo cannabis; of these, 32 completed all three smoking sessions. The study demonstrated an analgesic response to smoking cannabis with no significant difference between the low- and high-dose cigarettes. The study concluded that both low and high cannabis doses were efficacious in reducing neuropathic pain of diverse causes.

Disagreeable or unpleasant side effects were significantly more likely with high-dose cigarettes compared to low-dose or placebo, whereas there was no difference in these effects between low-dose and placebo sessions. There was no indication of mood changes (e.g., sadness, anxiety, fearfulness).

Marijuana as Analgesic, or Pain Reliever

This study ["Analgesic Efficacy of Smoked Cannabis"] used an experimental model of neuropathic pain to determine whether pain induced by the injection into the skin of capsaicin, a compound which is the "hot" ingredient in chili peppers, could be alleviated by smoked cannabis. Another aim of the study was to examine the effects of "dose" of cannabis, and the time course of pain relief. In a randomized double-blinded, placebo-controlled trial, volunteers smoked low, medium, and high dose cannabis (2%, 4%, 8% THC by weight) or placebo cigarettes.

Smoked cannabis was superior to placebo in reducing neuropathic pain of diverse causes.

The full results of this study were published in the journal *Anesthesiology*. Nineteen healthy volunteers were enrolled, and 15 completed all four smoking sessions. In brief, five minutes after cannabis exposure, there was no effect on capsaicin-induced pain at any dose. By 45 minutes after cannabis exposure there was a significant decrease in capsaicin-induced pain with the medium dose (4%) and a significant increase in pain with the high dose (8%). There was no significant effect seen with low dose (2%). There was a significant inverse relationship between pain perception and plasma THC. In summary, this study suggested that there may be a "therapeutic window" (or optimal dose) for smoked cannabis: low doses were not effective; medium doses decreased pain; and higher doses actually increased pain. These results suggest the mechanism(s) of cannabinoid analgesia are complex, in some ways like non-opioid pain relievers (e.g., aspirin, ibuprofen) and in others like opioids (e.g., morphine).

Marijuana for Spasticity in Multiple Sclerosis

The objective of this study ["Short-Term Effects of Cannabis Therapy on Spasticity in Multiple Sclerosis"] was to determine the potential for smoked cannabis to ameliorate marked muscle spasticity (chronic painful contraction of muscles), a severe and disabling symptom of multiple sclerosis. In a placebo-controlled, randomized clinical trial spasticity and global functioning was examined before and after treatment with smoked cannabis. Patients were allowed to continue their usual treatments for spasticity and pain while participating in the research.

The full results of this study are being submitted for publication. Initial results were presented at the meeting of the American College of Neuropsychopharmacology in 2007. Thirty patients with multiple sclerosis were enrolled. Compared to placebo cigarettes, cannabis was found to significantly reduce both an objective measure of spasticity and pain intensity. This study concluded that smoked cannabis was superior to placebo in reducing spasticity and pain in patients with multiple sclerosis, and provided some benefit beyond currently prescribed treatments. . . .

Results of CMCR studies support the likelihood that cannabis may represent a possible adjunctive avenue of treatment for certain difficult-to-treat conditions like neuropathic pain and spasticity.

Legalizing Medical Marijuana Is Not a Good Idea

Mark L. Kraus

Mark L. Kraus is a physician in Waterbury, Connecticut, and a member of the board of directors of the American Society of Addiction Medicine.

On behalf of the members of the Connecticut Chapter of the American Society of Addiction Medicine (ASAM) and the Connecticut State Medical Society I am delighted for this opportunity to voice our strong opposition to the continuing efforts being made in Connecticut to legislate marijuana for medical use. The members of ASAM have devoted their medical careers to further the development of treatment for addictive disorders, and the associated medical/psychiatric consequences. We are concerned that marijuana, a dangerous chemical, with life-altering properties, is being considered for use as a viable medicine.

Not a Conventional Drug

For those who are inclined to support medical use of marijuana, it is usually not the scientific evidence they consider, but only the unfounded self-reports of how marijuana relieved pain, chemotherapy-induced nausea and vomiting or HIV-AIDS wasting syndrome. We are deeply concerned that the myths surrounding the medical use of marijuana pose a grave danger to patients. Proponents of the legalization of medical marijuana create the impression that it is a reasonable alternative to conventional drugs. But unlike conventional drugs, smokable marijuana has not passed the rigorous scru-

Mark L. Kraus, "The Dangers of Legalizing Medical Marijuana: A Physician's Perspective," Testimony to the Connecticut Judiciary Committee, February 26, 2007. Courtesy of the Connecticut Joint Committee on Judiciary.

tiny of scientific investigation and has not been found safe and effective in treating pain, nausea and vomiting, or wasting syndrome.

1. Unlike most drugs administered orally, intravenously, intramuscularly, or by epidermal patch, marijuana is smoked. Like tobacco, smoked marijuana contains many of the same toxic or carcinogenic compounds that have been linked to lung cancer and emphysema. Current findings indicate that the evidence suggests that the marijuana cigarette, in contrast with the tobacco cigarette, delivers over four times the amount of tar and much higher concentration of polycyclic aromatic hydrocarbons, such as the carcinogen benzopyrene.

2. Marijuana smoke, like tobacco smoke, contains toxins and other foreign particulates that are known to cause inflammation in the lining of the lungs. Unlike tobacco smoke, marijuana smoke substantially reduced the alveolar macrophages, the lungs primary defense against infectious microorganisms, foreign substances and tumor cells. This is of particular concern for the immunocompromised HIV/AIDS patients or cancer patient, who is already at great risk for opportunistic lung infections. Though the evidence is by no means conclusive, chronic marijuana smoking may be a factor in the development of acute and chronic bronchitis, and increasing the risk of pneumonia.

3. Smoking marijuana can cause tachycardia and abrupt changes in blood pressure causing grave concern to those who have cardiovascular disease.

4. There is scientific evidence that long-term marijuana smoking alters the reproductive system.

A More Effective Treatment

Contemporary medicine and pharmacology are based on the application of scientific principles and the use of extensive clinical research to determine the safety and efficacy of a drug. For each symptom or disease advocated to be treated by smokable marijuana, there is a well-accepted, well-researched, and more effective treatment.

Among these drugs is Marinol (dronabinol), a synthetic version of the naturally occurring component of marijuana (THC or tetrahydrocannabinol), that is indicated to treat chronic pain, chemotherapy-related nausea and vomiting, and HIV/AIDS associated wasting syndrome. Marinol, however, unlike smokable marijuana, is a pure chemical compound that has been subjected to rigorous chemical research trials that have established its efficacy, safety, side effect profile, and proper dosing. Interestingly, the only known property Marinol lacks is the effect of creating "a high".

The Message Medical Marijuana Would Send

As addiction medicine specialists that are dedicated to the treatment of those afflicted by the disease—addiction—and to furthering science-based knowledge, we believe that these proposals to legislate the use of smokable marijuana as a medicine constitutes a far greater threat than many Americans truly realize. These proposals to use smoked marijuana as a medicine convey a mixed and ambiguous message to children, adolescents and adults. These messages undermine the many years invested by public health to prevent pre- and adolescent onset of the use of tobacco, marijuana, and other drugs. These proposals provide real contradictions that are not easily addressed or resolved in school and in family discussions, especially where the images of the marijuana user intrude into the day-to-day lives of these young people.

Current research indicates that the use of marijuana on a regular basis during adolescence is a strong marker for ensuring drug problems later in life. Young people are often misinformed and misled to believe that the use of marijuana is harmless and that you cannot become addicted. Nothing is further from the truth. There is clear evidence that the use of marijuana can result in dependency. These young people and other individuals dependent on this drug, will make the choice to use it in physically compromised situations, and will continue to use it putting their education, jobs, interpersonal relationships, and legal status at a significant risk.

To lower the level of current control of marijuana would only serve to exacerbate an already grave societal and medical problem.

An Unconscionable Proposal

In closing, I urge you to reject the proposal that would change the status quo by recognizing smokable marijuana as an accepted drug. As a practicing physician and a concerned member of my community, I can find no redeeming qualities derived from smoking a weed—marijuana.

It is unconscionable in this era, the 21st century, that our best effort to deliver effective pain relief, or to treat chemotherapy-induced nausea or vomiting, or treat HIV/AIDS wasting syndrome would consist of prescribing smokable marijuana. We must reject these efforts to give marijuana medical credibility by equating it with other more pharmacologically advanced drugs that have passed the rigors of scientific investigation/research and demonstrate significant efficacy in treating pain, nausea, and vomiting (chemotherapeutically induced) or HIV/AIDS wasting syndrome. It has no credibility. It has not passed the rigors of scientific investigation. It has not demonstrated significant efficacy in symptom relief. And, it causes harm.

As physicians we have a duty to follow the tenets of the Hippocratic Oath we have taken. "Do no harm." To lower the level of current control of marijuana would only serve to exacerbate an already grave societal and medical problem. To characterize those who do not support the legislation of medical marijuana as less than supportive of those who are "suffering" is a cynicism in the extreme. This campaign of self-serving political propaganda, misinformation, and deception must stop.

Crude Marijuana Is Not a Safe or Effective Medicine

Henry I. Miller

Henry I. Miller is a physician and a fellow at the Hoover Institution.

The medical marijuana controversy rages on. Is it a "medicine?" Does it work? Is it safe? Are claims of medical benefits merely a ploy for legalization?

The FDA's Position on Medical Marijuana

The FDA [Food and Drug Administration] weighed in several months ago [in 2006] by endorsing a multi-agency study that found "no animal or human data supported the safety or efficacy of marijuana for general medical use." This enraged those who claim that cannabis is an appropriate treatment for ailments from nausea and vomiting to muscle spasticity and intractable pain. They accused the FDA of elevating politics over science—more specifically, over the conclusions of a 1999 report from the Institute of Medicine (IOM), a branch of the prestigious National Academy of Sciences.

It also rubbed Charley Hooper the wrong way [in his August 18, 2006, article in *TCS Daily*]. However, his arguments are typical of the specious arguments in favor of using smoked marijuana—as opposed to purified, standardized drug preparations—for medicinal purposes. For example, he asserts that the FDA's statement, "no sound scientific studies supported medical use of marijuana . . . for general medical use," conflicts with the IOM report and other findings. The operative phrase here is *for general medical use*. No reputable group has made that claim.

Henry I. Miller, "The Straight Dope on 'Medical Marijuana,'" *TCS Daily*, September 1, 2006. www.ideasinactiontv.com/tcs_daily. Reproduced by permission.

In fact, the FDA's position both makes sense and is consistent with the requirements of the Federal Food, Drug, and Cosmetic Act. And in spite of claims to the contrary by cannabis supporters and much of the media, it is also consistent with the 1999 IOM report. The IOM's experts *rejected* the idea that crude herbal (usually smoked) cannabis had been shown to be a safe and effective medication for various medical conditions, concluded that there is "little future in smoked cannabis as a medically approved medication," and emphasized that smoked plant material is a crude drug delivery system that exposes patients to a significant number of harmful substances. They recommended smoked cannabis only for short-term use (less than 6 months), and only for patients who suffer from debilitating conditions like intractable pain or vomiting, who have failed on all other therapies, and who are under the close supervision of a physician and an institutional review board-type process. Finally, they predicted that "if there is any future of marijuana as a medicine, it lies in its isolated components, the cannabinoids and their synthetic derivatives," and called for clinical trials to develop "rapid-onset, reliable and safe delivery systems."

The Scientific and Legal Standards

The IOM's analysis is far from an endorsement of crude cannabis, in whatever form, as a safe and efficacious medicine that should be made available to patients for a wide variety of medical conditions, as is permitted in eleven states.

In the context of the IOM report and federal law, the FDA's position was perhaps inevitable. First, federal law requires that to be marketed, a drug must have been judged safe and effective by experts who have evaluated evidence obtained from well-controlled clinical trials.

Second, there is the question of what constitutes "evidence." Contrary to the implications of the news reports, it is not an amorphous collection of anecdotal reports and patient testimonials, but rather hard data arising out of carefully designed preclinical and clinical trials. Although there are some recent data from small safety and efficacy trials using smoked cannabis, as the IOM pointed out such trials are merely a first step towards the development of a suitably defined and tested pharmaceutical.

That brings us to a critical third point: What is a "medicine?" In order for a company to sell a drug, and a physician to prescribe it, it must be standardized by composition, formulation, and dose; have been tested for a particular medical condition in rigorous trials; and be administered by means of an appropriate delivery system.

There is no justification for treating cannabis differently from other pharmaceutical raw materials.

From these, as it were, first principles, it is clear that smoked marijuana will have great difficulty in meeting the required scientific and legal standards. There is insufficient evidence that smoked cannabis is a safe and effective medicine (leaving aside the question of whether the federal soldiers in "the war on drugs" have obstructed clinical testing). Different cannabis strains vary radically in cannabinoid composition and contaminants; plant materials may be contaminated with fungi, bacteria, pesticides, heavy metals and other substances; and there is no safe and reliable delivery system for crude cannabis products.

Natural, Synthetic, and Cannabis-Derived Drugs

All of this provides an answer to the question posed by Hooper in his article, "If the synthetic versions are so good, why hasn't the FDA embraced the natural version?" It's not standardizable, so it's not a medicine. Moreover, the synthetic versions are not, in fact, all that good. Both smoked marijuana and the synthetic versions of delta-9-tetrahydrocannabinol (THC) mentioned by Hooper are poorly tolerated by many patients for chronic use. But, as discussed below, there seems to be a better alternative on the horizon.

Finally, there is no justification for treating cannabis differently from other pharmaceutical raw materials. Other plant-derived drugs—morphine, codeine, and taxol, among many others—became available only after successfully passing through the FDA review process. The FDA recently issued a guidance document setting forth the path that botanically based products must take in order to gain regulatory approval, and cannabis must meet those requirements. If physicians and patients are ever to have meaningful access to cannabis's therapeutic potential, crude plant material should serve only as a substrate, the first step in the development of a modern medicine.

The FDA's position on medical marijuana does not forsake science in favor of politics, nor do regulators appear to be negatively disposed toward cannabis as the source of medicines. In January [2006], they approved an Investigational New Drug submission for a product called Sativex, a cannabis-derived drug that has been approved in Canada for the treatment of neuropathic pain in multiple sclerosis and that, although not yet fully licensed, is available by prescription in both Spain and the United Kingdom. More than 1,500 patients are currently using it for a variety of serious conditions under the supervision of their physicians.

A Cannaboid-Containing Drug

After reviewing the data, the FDA agreed to pivotal late-stage (Phase III) clinical trials of Sativex in the United States. The product has been standardized and tested in accordance with modern pharmaceutical standards. It is composed of a fixed ratio of cannabinoids (tetrahydrocannabinol and cannabidiol, a non-psychoactive cannabinoid, in a 1:1 ratio) and is administered by means of an oral spray that delivers the drug through the mucosa of the mouth. These elements appear to enlarge the "therapeutic window," better enabling patients to seek symptomatic relief without experiencing the kind of "high" that many view as an undesirable side effect.

Although it may be the presence of cannabidiol in Sativex that improves the risk/benefit profile, that compound is almost entirely absent from most herbal cannabis in the United States, which has been selected and bred to enhance the levels of tetrahydrocannabinol, THC, for recreational use. Another possible explanation for the minimal psychoactive effects is the spray delivery method, which prevents THC blood levels from rising too rapidly.

The availability of drugs like Sativex should (but won't) end the rancorous debate over medical marijuana in a way that would both benefit patients and satisfy the legal requirement that marketed medicines must be proven safe and effective. Even if it did, the issue of whether marijuana should be legalized as a recreational drug would remain.

Meanwhile, FDA officials must ensure that the testing and potential approval of cannabinoid-containing drugs are not hindered by political agendas or other nonscientific considerations, inside or outside the agency. For the benefit of patients in need, this is something about which the FDA, the "war on drugs" components of the government and other interested parties should strive to agree.

CHAPTER 2

Is Medical Marijuana Dangerous?

Overview: The Debate About the Dangers of Medical Marijuana

Jill U. Adams

Jill U. Adams is a science writer who reports on science and nature, research and policy, careers and education, community news, and parenting.

Marijuana is the most widely used illicit drug in the country—an estimated 25 million Americans smoked it within the last year [2007] and close to 100 million have smoked it at least once in their life, according to the most recent National Survey on Drug Use and Health by the federal Substance Abuse and Mental Health Services Administration.

Rates and severity of marijuana addiction pale in comparison to that of legal addictive drugs, alcohol and nicotine, according to the Advisory Council on the Misuse of Drugs, a panel of independent experts advising the British government, in a rare head-to-head, scientific comparison.

Yet, the fact is, recreational use can lead to addiction, and inhaling marijuana smoke is unhealthful for the lungs. Some researchers argue that marijuana may predispose heavy users to mental illnesses such as psychosis and depression.

Marijuana's Risks and Benefits

How big are these risks and how should they be measured against health benefits? "The FDA [Food and Drug Administration] has ruled that marijuana has no medical benefits, but its harms are well known and proven," says Tom Riley, a spokesman for the White House Office of National Drug Control Policy, referring to an April 2006 statement released by the FDA and several other federal agencies concluding that smoking marijuana was not of medicinal use.

For comparison's sake, Riley cites the prescription drug Vioxx. The FDA, he notes, pulled Vioxx off the market in spite of its proven efficacy, because it created problems in a small number of people.

Then, too, the number of people adversely affected by marijuana use is large, Riley says. "There are more teens in drug treatment for marijuana dependence than for alcohol or any other drug," he says.

Marijuana is a Schedule 1 drug by the Drug Enforcement Administration's Controlled Substances Act, a classification reserved for drugs carrying the highest risk for addiction and no medical benefit.

Scientists have reviewed the weed's risks and find them to be real, but small. Ten years ago, the Institute of Medicine reviewed the scientific evidence about marijuana at the request of the Office of National Drug Control Policy. The 1999 report states that "except for the harms associated with smoking, the adverse effects of marijuana use are within the range of effects tolerated for other medications."

In February [2008], the American College of Physicians, the nation's second-largest physicians group, released a position paper in support of medical-marijuana research, protecting doctors from criminal prosecution and rescheduling marijuana as a less harmful drug.

A British advisory group this year found no evidence to reclassify cannabis as a more harmful drug in that country. In contrast to the U.S., the U.K. [United Kingdom] puts cannabis in the lowest category (Class C) in terms of criminal penalties for possession or sale, although government officials are campaigning to move it to Class B.

To investigate the risks of marijuana, researchers typically use heavy marijuana smokers as subjects. Though such a study design may be convenient, it makes interpretation tricky because heavy users may have traits in common besides smoking pot. Thus, says psychologist and marijuana researcher Stanley Zammit of Cardiff University in Wales, it is not easy in these kinds of studies to separate out the contribution of marijuana to any measurable effect in the group.

Marijuana and Mental Illness

Claims of a link between marijuana use and psychotic episodes came under scrutiny after the U.K. downgraded cannabis from Class B to Class C in 2004. In 2007, Zammit was asked by England's Department of Health to survey the existing evidence to determine the long-term risks for mental illness from using cannabis. After researching the literature and including only those studies that satisfied certain criteria, he combined the results in a 2007 *Lancet* paper.

He concluded that marijuana use was associated with an increased risk of psychosis—ranging from self-reported symptoms such as delusions or hallucinations to clinically diagnosed schizophrenia.

The risk is small, he adds. Cannabis use was associated with a 40% increase in risk overall and up to a twofold increase in heavy users. Because the risk of any person developing psychosis in their lifetime is about 2% to 3%, cannabis use at worst increases that to 5%. "So 95% of the people are not going to get psychotic, even if they smoke on a daily basis," Zammit says.

Zammit adds that "the main limitation of these studies is that you can never be sure that it's the cannabis itself that's causing this risk." Heavy users of marijuana may differ from nonusers in other traits—including those that lead independently to increased drug use and risk of psychosis. The studies he reviewed tried to take into account this possibility but could not rule it out entirely.

The bottom line? "The evidence is probably strong enough that people should be aware of this risk," he says.

Even if it's real, the risk of developing psychosis because of marijuana use is smaller than with use of some other drugs—including legal ones such as cigarettes, says Mitch Earleywine, a psychologist at the State University of New York University at Albany.

[Psychiatry professor Igor] Grant says that numbers of schizophrenia cases have not increased since before the 1960s, when widespread marijuana use began. "The data are variable to be sure, but most studies have found that over the years the rate of schizophrenia has been stable or even declining," he says.

In an *American Journal of Psychiatry* study, 1,920 adults were assessed for marijuana use and depression and followed for 15 years. In those subjects who had no depressive symptoms at the study's start, marijuana abusers were four times more likely to develop depressive symptoms down the road. But Zammit, who reviewed this paper and 23 others in his 2007 *Lancet* paper, says the data overall are even murkier than for psychosis. Most of the studies he reviewed did not assess symptoms of depression before marijuana use, and so didn't rule out the idea that depression makes someone more likely to smoke marijuana—and not the other way around.

Marijuana's Effects on the Brain

A review of the scientific literature published in the *Journal of the International Neuropsychological Society* in 2003 looked at whether marijuana smoking had lasting effects on cognition after THC [tetrahydrocannabinol] has left the body. Marijuana use was found to have small effects on memory in long-term users—measured by asking subjects to recall words, for instance—but no differences were seen on attention, verbal skills and reaction time. "We were actually surprised," says Grant, an author on the study. Even if the marijuana itself wasn't causing such things, he expected marijuana users might have other less-than-healthful behaviors—they may drink a bit more, or use some other drugs, and "you might expect them to do a little worse."

How the drug affects adolescents is not completely resolved, but the data are more troubling.

A 2002 study published in the *Journal of the American Medical Association* found that a group of 51 heavy marijuana users (two joints per day) recalled two to three fewer words on average than nonusers in a memory test with a list of 15 words.

A second study, published in the *Archives of General Psychiatry* in 2001, found a similar deficit in 63 daily marijuana smokers who hadn't smoked for up to a week. After 28 days of not smoking marijuana the effect disappeared.

Studies on brain function and mental illness cited above were conducted in adult marijuana users. How the drug affects adolescents is not completely resolved, but the data are more troubling.

A 2000 paper in the *Journal of Addictive Diseases* recruited 58 marijuana users and found structural changes in the brains of those who had started smoking marijuana before age 17 but not in those who didn't start smoking until they were older.

"There's also a modest decrease in IQ if teens use heavily, though weekly users and folks who quit don't seem to show it," Earleywine says. Adolescence, he says, is a time when brain neurons are making oodles of new connections, and it's possible that a psychoactive drug such as marijuana may adversely influence that process.

Marijuana's Effects on the Lungs

Before it has any effect on the brain, marijuana smoke enters the body through the lungs. Dr. Donald Tashkin, professor of medicine at the UCLA [University of California, Los Angeles] David Geffen School of Medicine, has studied the pulmonary consequences of marijuana use for 25 years, recruiting a group of 280 heavy habitual pot smokers in the early 1980s, including some who also smoked cigarettes. (Subjects averaged three joints per day for an average of 15 years.) For comparison, he also recruited cigarette smokers who didn't use marijuana and people who didn't smoke anything.

Tashkin has done a number of studies over the decades comparing these groups. "I began with the hypothesis that regular smoking of marijuana would have an impact on the lungs qualitatively similar to the impact of regular tobacco smoking," he says. That's because the smoke of both plants are more similar than different.

Marijuana smokers differ from tobacco smokers.

Tashkin and his colleagues did find symptoms of chronic bronchitis in his marijuana-smoking group. In a 1987 study in the *American Review of Respiratory Diseases*, they reported that incidence of chronic cough, sputum production and wheezing was similar to that in cigarette smokers.

In a second study . . . published in the *American Journal of Respiratory and Critical Care Medicine* in 1998, examination of the airways and the cells lining the airways found swelling, redness and increased secretions in marijuana users. Biopsies showed "extensive, widespread damage to the mucosa," Tashkin says, similar to what was seen in tobacco users. "This is amazing, because the marijuana smokers average three joints a day, but the tobacco controls smoked 22 cigarettes, suggesting that on a cigarette-to-cigarette basis, marijuana may be more damaging."

Marijuana Smokers vs. Cigarette Smokers

But marijuana smokers differ from tobacco smokers in other, potentially more important ways, Tashkin adds. They do not seem to develop more serious consequences of cigarette smoking, namely chronic obstructive pulmonary disease (COPD)—the fourth-leading cause of death in the U.S., killing 130,000 people each year—or lung cancer, the most common cancer in Americans and responsible for an additional 160,000 annual deaths, according to 2005 statistics from the Centers for Disease Control and Prevention.

To study lung cancer, Tashkin looked at more than 600 lung cancer patients and more than 1,000 control patients matched for age, socioeconomic class, family history and other alcohol and drug use (along with many other potential influences).

The results, published in a 2006 paper in *Cancer Epidemiology, Biomarkers & Prevention*, found a large number of regular marijuana smokers were present in both groups, but statistically there were no more in the cancer group than control group, suggesting no association between marijuana use and lung cancer. Tobacco smokers, on the other hand, showed a dose-dependent increase in risk: with a 30%, 800% and 2,100% increased risk of lung cancer in those who smoked less than a pack, one to two packs or more than two packs per day, respectively.

Other studies have found increased cancer risk. A study of 79 lung cancer patients and 300 controls published in the *European Respiratory Journal* this year found a fivefold increased risk in the heaviest marijuana users (daily use for 10 years) and no effect in less heavy users.

But Tashkin says this conflicting report was much smaller in scale, having fewer than 20 subjects in the group of heaviest marijuana users. "My critique would be: It's a small study. I think that their small sample size is responsible for vastly inflated estimates," he says.

Marijuana Is Dangerous for Its Users and Others

U.S. Drug Enforcement Administration

The U.S. Drug Enforcement Administration is responsible for enforcing the controlled substances laws and regulations of the United States.

The campaign to legitimize what is called "medical" marijuana is based on two propositions: that science views marijuana as medicine, and that DEA [Drug Enforcement Administration] targets sick and dying people using the drug. Neither proposition is true. Smoked marijuana has not withstood the rigors of science—it is not medicine and it is not safe. DEA targets criminals engaged in cultivation and trafficking, not the sick and dying. No state has legalized the trafficking of marijuana, including the twelve states that have decriminalized certain marijuana use.

Smoked Marijuana Is Not Medicine

There is no consensus of medical evidence that smoking marijuana helps patients. Congress enacted laws against marijuana in 1970 based in part on its conclusion that marijuana has no scientifically proven medical value. The Food and Drug Administration (FDA) is the federal agency responsible for approving drugs as safe and effective medicine based on valid scientific data. FDA has not approved smoked marijuana for any condition or disease. The FDA noted that "there is currently sound evidence that smoked marijuana is harmful," and "that no sound scientific studies supported medical use of marijuana for treatment in the United States, and no animal or human data supported the safety or efficacy of marijuana for general medical use."

U.S. Drug Enforcement Administration, "The DEA Position on Marijuana," May 2006. www.justice.gov/dea. Courtesy of the U.S. Drug Enforcement Administration.

In 2001, the Supreme Court affirmed Congress's 1970 judgment about marijuana in *United States v. Oakland Cannabis Buyers' Cooperative et al.* (2001), which held that, given the absence of medical usefulness, medical necessity is not a defense to marijuana prosecution. Furthermore, in *Gonzales v. Raich* (2005), the Supreme Court reaffirmed that the authority of Congress to regulate the use of potentially harmful substances through the federal Controlled Substances Act includes the authority to regulate marijuana of a purely intrastate character, regardless of a state law purporting to authorize "medical" use of marijuana.

The DEA and the federal government are not alone in viewing smoked marijuana as having no documented medical value. Voices in the medical community likewise do not accept smoked marijuana as medicine:

- The American Cancer Society "does not advocate inhaling smoke, nor the legalization of marijuana," although the organization does support carefully controlled clinical studies for alternative delivery methods, specifically a THC [tetrahydrocannabinol] skin patch.

- The American Academy of Pediatrics (AAP) believes that "[a]ny change in the legal status of marijuana, even if limited to adults, could affect the prevalence of use among adolescents." While it supports scientific research on the possible medical use of cannabinoids as opposed to smoked marijuana, it opposes the legalization of marijuana.

- The National Multiple Sclerosis Society (NMSS) states that studies done to date "have not provided convincing evidence that marijuana benefits people with MS [multiple sclerosis]," and thus marijuana is not a recommended treatment. Furthermore, the NMSS warns that the "long-term use of marijuana may be associated with significant serious side effects."

- The British Medical Association (BMA) voiced extreme concern that downgrading the criminal status of marijuana would "mislead" the public into believing that the drug is safe. The BMA maintains that marijuana "has been linked to greater risk of heart disease, lung cancer, bronchitis and emphysema." The 2004 Deputy Chairman of the BMA's Board of Science said that "[t]he public must be made aware of the harmful effects we know result from smoking this drug."

- The American Academy of Pediatrics asserted that with regard to marijuana use, "from a public health perspective, even a small increase in use, whether attributable to increased availability or decreased perception of risk, would have significant ramifications."

A Landmark Study

In 1999, the Institute of Medicine (IOM) released a landmark study reviewing the supposed medical properties of marijuana. The study is frequently cited by "medical" marijuana advocates, but in fact severely undermines their arguments.

- After release of the IOM study, the principal investigators cautioned that the active compounds in marijuana may have medicinal potential and therefore should be researched further. However, the study concluded that "there is little future in smoked marijuana as a medically approved medication."

- For some ailments, the IOM found " . . . potential therapeutic value of cannabinoid drugs, primarily THC, for pain relief, control of nausea and vomiting, and appetite stimulation." However, it pointed out that "[t]he effects of cannabinoids on the symptoms studied are generally modest, and in most cases there are more effective medications [than smoked marijuana]."

- The study concluded that, at best, there is only anecdotal information on the medical benefits of smoked marijuana for some ailments, such as muscle spasticity. For other ailments, such as epilepsy and glaucoma, the study found no evidence of medical value and did not endorse further research.

- The IOM study explained that "smoked marijuana . . . is a crude THC delivery system that also delivers harmful substances." In addition, "plants contain a variable mixture of biologically active compounds and cannot be expected to provide a precisely defined drug effect." Therefore, the study concluded that "there is little future in smoked marijuana as a medically approved medication."

- The principal investigators explicitly stated that using smoked marijuana in clinical trials "should not be designed to develop it as a licensed drug, but should be a stepping stone to the development of new, safe delivery systems of cannabinoids."

Thus, even scientists and researchers who believe that certain active ingredients in marijuana may have potential medicinal value openly discount the notion that smoked marijuana is or can become "medicine."

Legalization of marijuana, no matter how it begins, will come at the expense of our children and public safety.

DEA has approved and will continue to approve research into whether THC has any medicinal use. As of May 8, 2006, DEA had registered every one of the 163 researchers who requested to use marijuana in studies and who met Department of Health and Human Services standards. One of those researchers, the Center for Medicinal Cannabis Research (CMCR), conducts studies "to ascertain the general medical safety and efficacy of cannabis and cannabis products and examine alternative forms of cannabis administration." The CMCR currently has 11 ongoing studies involving marijuana and the efficacy of cannabis and cannabis compounds as they relate to medical conditions such as HIV, cancer pain, MS, and nausea.

At present, however, the clear weight of the evidence is that smoked marijuana is harmful. No matter what medical condition has been studied, other drugs already approved by the FDA, such as Marinol—a pill form of synthetic THC—have been proven to be safer and more effective than smoked marijuana.

Dangers to the User and Others

Legalization of marijuana, no matter how it begins, will come at the expense of our children and public safety. It will create dependency and treatment issues, and open the door to use of other drugs, impaired health, delinquent behavior, and drugged drivers.

This is not the marijuana of the 1970s; today's marijuana is far more powerful. Average THC levels of seized marijuana rose from less than one per cent in the mid-1970s to a national average of over eight per cent in 2004. And the potency of "B.C. Bud" [cannabis grown in British Columbia, Canada] is roughly twice the national average—ranging from 15 per cent to as high as 25 per cent THC content.

- Adolescents are at highest risk for marijuana addiction, as they are "three times more likely than adults to develop dependency" [according to the Seattle *Post-Intelligencer*]. This is borne out by the fact that treatment admission rates for adolescents reporting marijuana as the primary substance of abuse increased from 32 to 65 per cent between 1993 and 2003. More young people ages 12–17 entered treatment in 2003 for marijuana dependency than for alcohol and all other illegal drugs combined.

• "[R]esearch shows that use of [marijuana] can lead to dependence. Some heavy users of marijuana develop withdrawal symptoms when they have not used the drug for a period of time. Marijuana use, in fact, is often associated with behavior that meets the criteria for substance dependence established by the American Psychiatric Association" [according to the Office of National Drug Control Policy].

• Of the 19.1 million Americans aged 12 or older who used illicit drugs in the past 30 days in 2004, 14.6 million used marijuana, making it the most commonly used illicit drug in 2004.

• Among all ages, marijuana was the most common illicit drug responsible for treatment admissions in 2003, accounting for 15 per cent of all admissions—outdistancing heroin, the next most prevalent cause.

• In 2003, 20 per cent (185,239) of the 919,833 adults admitted to treatment for illegal drug abuse cited marijuana as their primary drug of abuse.

A Precursor to Abuse of Other Drugs

• Marijuana is a frequent precursor to the use of more dangerous drugs and signals a significantly enhanced likelihood of drug problems in adult life. The *Journal of the American Medical Association* reported, based on a study of 300 sets of twins, "that marijuana-using twins were four times more likely than their siblings to use cocaine and crack cocaine, and five times more likely to use hallucinogens such as LSD."

- Long-term studies on patterns of drug usage among young people show that very few of them use other drugs without first starting with marijuana. For example, one study found that among adults (age 26 and older) who had used cocaine, 62 per cent had initiated marijuana use before age 15. By contrast, less than one per cent of adults who never tried marijuana went on to use cocaine.

- Columbia University's National Center on Addiction and Substance Abuse reports that teens who used marijuana at least once in the last month are 13 times likelier than other teens to use another drug like cocaine, heroin, or methamphetamine, and almost 26 times likelier than those teens who have never used marijuana to use another drug.

- Marijuana use in early adolescence is particularly ominous. Adults who were early marijuana users were found to be five times more likely to become dependent on any drug, eight times more likely to use cocaine in the future, and fifteen times more likely to use heroin later in life.

- In 2003, 3.1 million Americans aged 12 or older used marijuana daily or almost daily in the past year. Of those daily marijuana users, nearly two-thirds [according to the Department of Health and Human Services] "used at least one other illicit drug in the past 12 months." More than half (53.3 per cent) of daily marijuana users were also dependent on or abused alcohol or another illicit drug compared to those who were nonusers or used marijuana less than daily.

- Health care workers, legal counsel, police and judges indicate that marijuana is a typical precursor to methamphetamine. For instance, Nancy Kneeland, a substance abuse counselor in Idaho, pointed out that "in almost all cases meth users began with alcohol and pot."

Mental and Physical Health Issues

- John Walters, director of the Office of National Drug Control Policy; Charles G. Curie, administrator of the Substance Abuse and Mental Health Services Administration; and experts and scientists from leading mental health organizations joined together in May 2005 to warn parents about the mental health dangers marijuana poses to teens. According to several recent studies, marijuana use has been linked with depression and suicidal thoughts, in addition to schizophrenia. These studies report that weekly marijuana use among teens doubles the risk of developing depression and triples the incidence of suicidal thoughts.

- Dr. Andrew Campbell, a member of the New South Wales (Australia) Mental Health Review Tribunal, published a study in 2005 which revealed that four out of five individuals with schizophrenia were regular cannabis users when they were teenagers. Between 75–80 per cent of the patients involved in the study used cannabis habitually between the ages of 12 and 21. In addition, a laboratory-controlled study by Yale scientists, published in 2004, found that THC "transiently induced a range of schizophrenia-like effects in healthy people."

- Smoked marijuana has also been associated with an increased risk of the same respiratory symptoms as tobacco, including coughing, phlegm production, chronic bronchitis, shortness of breath and wheezing. Because cannabis plants are contaminated with a range of fungal spores, smoking marijuana may also increase the risk of respiratory exposure by infectious organisms (i.e., molds and fungi).

- Marijuana takes the risks of tobacco and raises them: marijuana smoke contains more than 400 chemicals and increases the risk of serious health consequences, including lung damage.

- According to two studies [reported by Reuters], marijuana use narrows arteries in the brain, "similar to patients with high blood pressure and dementia," and may explain why memory tests are difficult for marijuana users. In addition, "chronic consumers of cannabis lose molecules called CB1 receptors in the brain's arteries," leading to blood flow problems in the brain which can cause memory loss, attention deficits, and impaired learning ability.

- Carleton University researchers published a study in 2005 showing that current marijuana users who smoke at least five "joints" per week did significantly worse than nonusers when tested on neurocognition tests such as processing speed, memory, and overall IQ.

Delinquent Behaviors and Drugged Driving

- In 2002, the percentage of young people engaging in delinquent behaviors "rose with [the] increasing frequency of marijuana use." For example, according to a National Survey on Drug Use and Health (NSDUH) report, 42.2 per cent of youths who smoked marijuana 300 or more days per year and 37.1 per cent of those who did so 50-99 days took part in serious fighting at school or work. Only 18.2 per cent of those who did not use marijuana in the past year engaged in serious fighting.

- A large shock trauma unit conducting an ongoing study found that 17 per cent (one in six) of crash victims tested positive for marijuana. The rates were slightly higher for crash victims under the age of eighteen, 19 per cent of whom tested positive for marijuana.

- In a study of high school classes in 2000 and 2001, about 28,000 seniors each year admitted that they were in at least one accident after using marijuana.

- Approximately 15 per cent of teens reported driving under the influence of marijuana. This is almost equal to the percentage of teens who reported driving under the influence of alcohol (16 per cent).

- A study of motorists pulled over for reckless driving showed that, among those who were not impaired by alcohol, 45 per cent tested positive for marijuana.

- The National Highway Traffic Safety Administration (NHTSA) has found that marijuana significantly impairs one's ability to safely operate a motor vehicle. According to its report, "[e]pidemiology data from road traffic arrests and fatalities indicate that after alcohol, marijuana is the most frequently detected psychoactive substance among driving populations." Problems reported include: decreased car handling performance, inability to maintain headway, impaired time and distance estimation, increased reaction times, sleepiness, lack of motor coordination, and impaired sustained vigilance.

The Consequences of Marijuana-Impaired Driving

- The driver of a charter bus, whose 1999 accident resulted in the death of 22 people, had been fired from bus companies in 1989 and 1996 because he tested positive for marijuana four times. A federal investigator confirmed [in the *Orange County Register* in May 1999] a report that the driver "tested positive for marijuana when he was hospitalized Sunday after the bus veered off a highway and plunged into an embankment."

- In April 2002, four children and the driver of a van died when the van hit a concrete bridge abutment after veering off the freeway. Investigators reported that the children nicknamed the driver "Smokey" because he regularly smoked marijuana. The driver was found at the crash scene with marijuana in his pocket.

- A former nurse's aide was convicted in 2003 of murder and sentenced to 50 years in prison for hitting a homeless man with her car and driving home with his mangled body [according to the Fort Worth *Star-Telegram*] "lodged in the windshield." The incident happened after a night of drinking and taking drugs, including marijuana. After arriving home, the woman parked her car, with the man still lodged in the windshield, and left him there until he died.

- In April 2005, an eight-year-old boy was killed when he was run over by an unlicensed 16-year-old driver who police believed had been smoking marijuana just before the accident.

- In 2001, George Lynard was convicted of driving with marijuana in his bloodstream, causing a head-on collision that killed a 73-year-old man and a 69-year-old woman. Lynard appealed this conviction because he allegedly had a "valid prescription" for marijuana [according to the Associated Press]. A Nevada judge agreed with Lynard and granted him a new trial. The case has been appealed to the Nevada Supreme Court.

- Duane Baehler, 47, of Tulsa, Oklahoma, was "involved in a fiery crash that killed his teenage son" in 2003 [according to the Associated Press]. Police reported that Baehler had methamphetamine, cocaine and marijuana in his system at the time of the accident.

Marijuana also creates hazards that are not always predictable. In August 2004, two Philadelphia firefighters died battling a fire that started because of tangled wires and lamps used to grow marijuana in a basement closet.

Marijuana's Dangers Make It a Poor Candidate for Medicine

National Institute on Drug Abuse

The National Institute on Drug Abuse—part of the National Institutes of Health, a component of the US Department of Health and Human Services—supports and disseminates research on drug abuse and addiction.

In 2008, nearly 26 million Americans (10%) aged 12 or older reported abusing marijuana within the past year and more than 4 million met DSM-IV [the American Psychiatric Association's fourth edition of *Diagnostic and Statistical Manual of Mental Disorders*] criteria for abuse or dependence (addiction).

According to NIDA's [National Institute on Drug Abuse's] Monitoring the Future study, while marijuana use among 8th, 10th, and 12th graders showed a consistent decline starting in the mid-1990s, this decline has stalled in the past few years. Past month use was reported by 6.5% of 8th graders, 15.9% of 10th graders, and 20.6% of 12th graders, or 1 in 5 seniors. Thus, marijuana use does not reflect the continuing downward trend occurring with cigarettes. Among 12th graders, 5.2% are daily marijuana users, a rate unchanged since peak years in 2002 and 2003 (6%).

Marijuana's Effects

Marijuana is derived from plants containing more than 400 chemical constituents. Tetrahydrocannabinol (THC) is the main psychoactive ingredient in marijuana. It binds to cannabinoid (CB) receptors, widely distributed throughout the nervous system, and other parts of the body. In the brain CB

National Institute on Drug Abuse, "Marijuana," *Topics in Brief*, May 2010, pp. 1–2. Courtesy of the National Institute on Drug Abuse.

receptors are found in high concentrations in areas that influence pleasure, memory, thought, concentration, sensory and time perception, appetite, pain, and movement coordination. This is why marijuana can have wide-ranging effects, including:

- Impaired short-term memory (memory of recent events)—making it hard to learn and retain information, particularly complex tasks

- Slowed reaction time and impaired motor coordination—throwing off athletic performance, impairing driving skills, and increasing the risk of injuries

- Altered judgment and decision making—possibly leading to high-risk sexual behaviors, that could lead to the spread of HIV or other sexually transmitted diseases

- Increased heart rate by 20–100%—may increase the risk of heart attack, especially in otherwise vulnerable individuals

- Altered mood—euphoria, calmness, or in high doses anxiety, paranoia

- *Exposure during critical developmental periods*: From animal research, THC exposure pre- or perinatally or during adolescence can alter brain development, particularly in areas related to mood, reward, and executive function (e.g., cognitive flexibility)

Long-term marijuana abuse:

- Risk of addiction

- Poorer educational outcomes and job performance, diminished life satisfaction

- Respiratory problems—chronic cough, bronchitis

- Risk of psychosis in vulnerable individuals

- Cognitive impairment persisting beyond the time of intoxication

Marijuana Dependency and Addiction

People who are *dependent* on marijuana frequently have other comorbid mental disorders. Population studies reveal evidence of an association between cannabis use and increased risk of schizophrenia and, to a lesser extent, depression, and anxiety. There are now sufficient data indicating that marijuana may trigger the onset or relapse of schizophrenia in people predisposed to it, perhaps also intensifying their symptoms.

Long-term marijuana use can lead to addiction; that is, people use the drug compulsively even though it interferes with family, school, work, and recreational activities. According to the National Survey on Drug Use and Health, in 2008 of the estimated 7 million Americans classified with dependence on or abuse of illicit drugs, 4 million were dependent on or abused marijuana. In 2007, 15.8% of people entering drug abuse treatment programs reported marijuana as their primary drug of abuse (61% of those under 15), representing nearly 288,000 treatment admissions. Along with craving, withdrawal symptoms such as irritability, sleeping problems, and anxiety can make it difficult for long-term marijuana smokers to quit. Past research has shown that approximately 9% of people who use marijuana may become dependent. The risk of addiction goes up to about 1 in 6 among those who start using as adolescents, and 25–50% of daily users.

Marijuana is an unlikely medication candidate.

While no medication currently exists to treat marijuana addiction, a number of behavioral therapies have been shown to work: motivational incentives (awarding vouchers or "prizes" for abstinence); motivational enhancement (helping people increase their personal motivation to quit); and cognitive behavioral therapy (teaching patients new coping strategies).

Research has found that a cannabinoid antagonist can block marijuana's subjective effects. However, this medication does not have FDA [Food and Drug Administration] approval in this country (it is approved for treating obesity in Europe), and compliance may be an issue because of the potential for depression/anxiety associated with its use. Also, preliminary research has shown that oral THC combined with lofexidine, (historically used to treat hypertension) helps to ease symptoms associated with withdrawal. Research regarding medications for marijuana addiction is ongoing.

Marijuana as Medicine

Marijuana is not an FDA approved medicine, although 14 states have currently legalized its medical use. There are data supporting marijuana's potential therapeutic value for symptoms including pain relief, control of nausea, and appetite stimulation. However, there are several reasons why marijuana is an unlikely medication candidate: (1) it is an unpurified plant containing numerous chemicals with unknown health effects, (2) it is typically consumed by smoking further contributing to potential adverse effects, and its non-patentable status makes it an unattractive investment for pharmaceutical companies.

The promise lies instead in medications developed from marijuana's active components, the cannabinoids, or (perhaps less so) for the development of alternative delivery systems for marijuana consumption. The goal in developing purified or synthetic derivatives of marijuana's active components is to design more tailored medications with improved risk/benefit profiles. A number of cannabinoid-based medications are under investigation, with some already approved, that harness the new knowledge and therapeutic potential of this system for treating: pain associated with multiple sclerosis, obesity and metabolic disorders, neurodegenerative diseases, and addiction.

The Objections to Medical Marijuana's Safety Are Unfounded

Marijuana Policy Project

The Marijuana Policy Project is an organization working to reform marijuana laws by legalizing medical marijuana and eliminating criminal penalties for all marijuana use.

Objection: There is little trustworthy evidence that smoked marijuana actually works.

Reply: In a White House-commissioned 1999 report, the National Academy of Sciences' Institute of Medicine [IOM], in a review of the current science at the time, found extensive scientific evidence verifying that marijuana has medical value for patients suffering from pain, nausea, appetite loss, and other symptoms of illnesses such as cancer, multiple sclerosis, and HIV/AIDS. The IOM report stated, "Nausea, appetite loss, pain, and anxiety are all afflictions of wasting and all can be mitigated by marijuana ... there are patients with debilitating symptoms for whom smoked marijuana might provide relief." Subsequent studies since the 1999 Institute of Medicine report, including randomized, double-blind, placebo-controlled clinical trials, continue to show the therapeutic value of marijuana in treating a wide array of debilitating medical conditions, including relieving medication side effects and thus improving the likelihood that patients will adhere to life-prolonging treatments for HIV/AIDS and hepatitis C. Marijuana was also shown to be effective at alleviating HIV/AIDS neuropathy, a painful condition for which there are no FDA [Food and Drug Administration]-approved treatments. That is why, in January 2008, the American College of Physi-

Marijuana Policy Project, "Potential Objections to Medical Marijuana," November 2008, pp. 1–6 www.mpp.org. Reproduced by permission.

cians—the second-largest physician group in the country—called for marijuana to be reclassified under federal law to allow physician prescriptions, citing "marijuana's proven efficacy at treating certain symptoms and its relatively low toxicity."

The Health Consequences of Marijuana Use

Objection: Marijuana is an addictive drug that poses significant health consequences to its users.

Reply: Marijuana and cannabinoids have a generally excellent safety profile. Unlike many medicines, acute lethal overdoses of marijuana have not been reported, and research has not documented increased mortality attributable to chronic use. Concerns about immunological impairment have not been borne out in research with AIDS patients. No medications are without risk; however, medical marijuana is relatively benign compared to many routinely prescribed drugs. The American College of Physicians noted marijuana's "relatively low toxicity" in its January 2008 statement. Further, the American Public Health Association's official position statement on medical marijuana states, "[M]arijuana has an extremely wide acute margin of safety for use under physician supervision and cannot cause lethal reactions ... greater harm is caused by the legal consequences of its prohibition than possible risks of medicinal use." And, in its 1999 study, the Institute of Medicine concluded that, "Compared to most other drugs ... dependence among marijuana users is relatively rare."

Objection: Smoked marijuana is a known carcinogen with hundreds of well-documented negative effects.

Reply: In fact, the largest and most well-controlled studies have consistently found that marijuana smokers don't have higher rates of lung cancer or other typically tobacco-related cancers. A 2006 NIDA [National Institute on Drug Abuse]-funded case-control study co-authored by Dr. Donald Tashkin—one of the world's foremost experts on the respiratory effects of illicit drugs—found no increased risk of lung cancer among even the heaviest marijuana smokers. Indeed, there was a trend toward lower lung cancer risk among even heavy marijuana smokers as compared to nonsmokers, though the difference did not reach statistical significance. One possible explanation for this is the growing body of evidence documenting the antitumor actions of cannabinoids. Also, a 1997 Kaiser Permanente epidemiological study of 65,000 subjects showed no increase in lung or other tobacco-related cancers due to marijuana smoking, suggesting the potential of a favorable risk/benefit ratio for smoked medical marijuana in some chronic and/or painful conditions. It is worth noting in this context that the phrase "smoked marijuana" is a red herring. Marijuana need not be administered by smoking: It can be taken in food, tea, or through a smokeless vaporizer. Vaporization technology, discussed in the American College of Physicians' position paper, has been shown to achieve the drug delivery benefits of inhalation—rapid action and ease of dose titration—without the harmful combustion products contained in smoke.

Objection: Marijuana can cause schizophrenia.

Reply: Concerns have been raised in recent years regarding associations between marijuana use and acute psychosis and schizophrenia. While marijuana users have higher rates of psychotic symptoms or diagnosed psychosis than nonusers, the relative risk remains modest, and increased rates of marijuana use in the U.S. and Australia during the 1970s and 1980s did not lead to increased incidence of schizophrenia. Overall, the evidence suggests that marijuana use can precipitate psychosis in vulnerable individuals but is unlikely to cause the illness in otherwise normal persons. Use of cannabinoids in patients with a family or personal history of psychosis should generally be avoided until more is known.

Harm to Doctors and Patients

Objection: The mere existence of medical marijuana access laws puts both patient and physician in harm's way.

Reply: Medical marijuana access promotes physician autonomy to recommend the evidence-based medical treatment that is best for a patient, without legal punishment. Organized medicine should recognize the difference between licensing a drug for marketing and simply exempting patients using marijuana in state-sanctioned programs under the advice and supervision of a physician from criminal prosecution. Federal courts have upheld the right of physicians to recommend marijuana to patients, and physicians in the 13 medical marijuana states who follow appropriate standards of care when recommending marijuana have not experienced difficulties.

Objection: There is no clear reason why the American Medical Association [AMA] and other physician groups should support patient protection for legitimate medical marijuana users in the 13 state-sanctioned programs.

Reply: Existing AMA policy already affirms the protection of physicians practicing in medical marijuana states from federal prosecution for discussing and recommending medical marijuana to their patients. It does not, however, extend protection to the patients themselves in medical marijuana states, an important omission that warrants addressing by the AMA. In addition to arrest, fines, and confiscation of property and legally obtained supplies of medical marijuana, patients and their families have been subjected to DEA [Drug Enforcement Administration] "SWAT team" style invasions of their homes and the sudden discontinuation of their medical marijuana treatment. This can lead to exacerbation of chronic pain, wasting, and other serious medical conditions previously controlled by medical marijuana. Subjecting seriously ill patients to arrest and prosecution constitutes cruel and unusual punishment, which is why the editor in chief of the *New England Journal of Medicine* called the federal ban on the medical use of marijuana "misguided, heavy-handed, and inhumane." Federal law makes no distinction between those who possess or grow marijuana for medical purposes and those who are using it recreationally: the same penalties apply. The possession of a single marijuana cigarette can result in a sentence of up to one year, while the cultivation of a single marijuana plant can produce a sentence of up to five years.

Public opinion polls—and actual votes at the ballot box—show that support for medical marijuana is overwhelming.

The View of Physicians and the Public

Objection: We don't know what the general physician sentiment on this issue is.

Reply: In a 2005 poll conducted by HCD Research and the Muhlenberg College Institute of Public Opinion of 922 U.S. office-based physicians weighted by specialty and geography, 74% disagreed that "the federal government should be able to prosecute those who use, grow, or obtain marijuana prescribed or recommended by their doctor for chronic pain within the guidelines of state law."

Objection: Supporting any form of medical marijuana access is politically risky for physician organizations.

Reply: Across the country and with increasing frequency, public opinion polls—and actual votes at the ballot box—show that support for medical marijuana is overwhelming, steadily rising, and cuts across demographic and party lines. A 2004 AARP [American Association of Retired Persons] poll showed that 72% of seniors support medical marijuana, and a 2005 Gallup poll found that 78% of Americans support "making marijuana legally available for doctors to prescribe in order to reduce pain and suffering." Not one of the state medical marijuana laws passed since 1996 has been repealed. Indeed, when legislatures have made changes to these laws, it has generally been to extend and expand them. For example, in 2002, Maine increased the amount of medical marijuana that patients are allowed to possess. In 2007, Vermont expanded the list of conditions covered under the program and increased the number of marijuana plants that patients could legally grow. These are not the sorts of actions that legislators take when a law is unpopular.

Objection: The American Medical Association is a leader in organized medicine and [its] policy on medical marijuana is clear, consistent, and sufficient at this time.

There is no published evidence indicating that the medical use of marijuana has led to an increase in motor vehicle accidents.

Reply: The Connecticut newspaper *Guilford Courier* interviewed AMA spokesperson Robert Mills (Office of Media Relations) and reported on July 15, 2005, that "the AMA recommends keeping marijuana [unchanged] as a controlled substance 'pending the outcomes of studies to prove the application and efficacy of marijuana and other related cannabinoids'" but, in contrast, Mills and an American Cancer Society spokesman "both mentioned that patients afflicted with cancer and other painful medical conditions should not be prosecuted for trying to alleviate their suffering." Furthermore, the AMA is a member organization of the Accreditation Council for Continuing Medical Education (ACCME). Medical colleges and hospitals accredited by the ACCME have awarded AMA PRA [Physician's Recognition Award] Category 1 credits to physicians attending conferences and CME [continuing medical education] events focusing on medical marijuana clinical therapeutics and research. The AMA defines the content of CME as "the body of knowledge and skills generally recognized and accepted by the profession as within the basic medical sciences, the discipline of clinical medicine, and the provision of health care to the public."

Dangerous Side Effects of Marijuana Use

Objection: Marijuana use can cause psychosis in some people and, if a patient who had a recommendation from a physician commits a violent act, that physician could be subject to criminal prosecution.

Reply: Thousands of physicians have recommended medical marijuana to tens of thousands of patients in the 13 states where it is sanctioned by law. There have been no recorded cases of a psychotic reaction by a patient to marijuana that have resulted in a physician being put at legal or criminal risk for issuing such a recommendation. A great many prescription medicines can cause adverse psychiatric reactions, some much more commonly than the putative link between marijuana and psychosis. This is the sort of risk that physicians manage every day by appropriately evaluating, screening, and monitoring patients.

Objection: If wider access were allowed to medical marijuana for legitimate patients, there would be an increase in the amount of marijuana-related car crashes and fatalities.

Reply: As with the use of any medication, common sense and personal responsibility must prevail. Literally hundreds of prescription and over-the-counter drugs—taken every day by millions of Americans—can cause drowsiness or slowed reactions and should not be used while driving. We do not deny patients who need these medicines the relief they need because driving while taking them is contraindicated; instead, we expect them to use common sense. Medical marijuana patients should be held accountable to the same standards and laws as those who take any medicine with the potential to impair coordination and decision making. One-fifth of the U.S. population now lives in states with medical marijuana laws, but there is no published evidence indicating that the medical use of marijuana has led to an increase in motor vehicle accidents in any of these states.

Objection: Increased medical marijuana access would lead to decreases in workplace productivity.

Reply: There is no reason to believe that this is the case, and some reason to believe that the opposite is true. No medical marijuana law requires employers to accommodate marijuana use in the workplace. Many patients, however, report that marijuana, by providing improved relief of nausea, pain, loss of sleep, and other symptoms, allows them to work more productively than they could before beginning a medical marijuana regimen. And some have found that their marijuana regimen actually allowed them to return to work, when without using marijuana they had been too ill to do so.

Medical marijuana is a safe alternative for patients whose other options are not as reliable or effective.

The Social Harms of Marijuana Use

Objection: Affirmative positions supporting medical marijuana endanger our children and encourage abuse of the drug.

Reply: Of the 13 medical marijuana states, 11 now have data on teen marijuana use from both before and after the medical marijuana laws were passed. Adolescent marijuana use has not risen in a single one of these states. Instead, it has declined since medical marijuana became legal. For example, in California—the state where tales of abuse appear to be most common—the state-sponsored California Student Survey found that 34.2 percent of ninth graders reported having used marijuana in the past six months in 1995-96, the last survey before California's medical marijuana law, Proposition 215 [the Compassionate Use Act of 1996], passed. This represented a near-doubling from the 1991-92 survey. Teen marijuana use began to decline in the 1997-98 survey, the first conducted after Prop. 215 passed. By 1999-2000, past-six-months marijuana use by ninth graders had plunged to 19.2

percent, and it has declined even further since then. The American College of Physicians notes, "Opiates are highly addictive yet medically effective substances and are classified as Schedule II substances," but "there is no evidence to suggest that medical use of opiates has increased perception that their illicit use is safe or acceptable."

Objection: Marijuana is a gateway drug to harder substances, and therefore medical marijuana use will lead to dangerous drug use.

Reply: In science, the distinction between correlation and causation is crucial. The "gateway theory" has been roundly debunked by many credible sources. According to a 2006 study commissioned by the British Parliament, "the gateway theory has little evidence to support it despite copious research." The Institute of Medicine has concluded, "There is no evidence that marijuana serves as a stepping stone [to other drugs] on the basis of its particular physiological effect." The American College of Physicians noted in February 2008, "Marijuana has not been proven to be the cause or even the most serious predictor of serious drug abuse. It is also important to note that the data on marijuana's role in illicit drug use progression only pertains to its nonmedical use." In any case, it is absurd on its face to cite a supposed "gateway effect" for patients who are already routinely prescribed opiates and other highly addictive, potentially deadly narcotics. Medical marijuana is a safe alternative for patients whose other options are not as reliable or effective.

Objection: Medical marijuana laws create opportunities for diversion to illegal markets.

Reply: Recent press reports have indicated that the DEA is continuing to close down medical marijuana dispensaries ("buyers' clubs"). Reports emphasize the large volume of marijuana being cultivated by some dispensaries and the risk of diversion to illegal sales outside of the medical marijuana patient community. While these risks are not trivial, neither is the ongoing problem of diversion of prescription drugs to illicit uses—and yet we do not deny patients who need these drugs appropriate relief because of such abuse. The best way to ensure that medical marijuana is not diverted to illicit uses is through appropriate regulation and control, but federal law enforcement efforts have actually hampered and interfered with attempts by state and local governments to implement such controls. The AMA could encourage state and local governments to develop stronger systems of licensing and oversight of medical marijuana production. It could also call upon the federal government either to participate constructively in such regulation or get out of the way of state efforts to do so.

The Need for More Research

Objection: The American Medical Association and others already have pro-research positions on medical marijuana.

Reply: The current research climate for marijuana has created a significant chilling effect for researchers wanting to pursue FDA-approved clinical and basic research on the safety and efficacy of medical marijuana. While existing AMA policy recommends that NIDA should provide medical marijuana for all FDA-approved clinical and basic research studies in the U.S., this recommendation has gone unheeded by NIDA, which has refused to supply medical marijuana to several privately funded, FDA-approved research projects and has delayed initiation of other projects (including those approved and funded by NIDA) for several years. A more strongly worded position that specifically recommends marijuana's reclassification under federal law and/or the licensing of private medical marijuana production facilities that meet all regulatory requirements to produce pharmaceutical-grade marijuana for use exclusively in federally approved research would provide a solution to the current no-win situation. It is entirely appropriate for organized medicine to respond to the current legal limbo to help create a positive climate for increased research.

Objection: There have been many federally sanctioned studies on the medical use of marijuana in the past decade. These studies are continuing today, and they will continue in the future.

Reply: On the contrary, only a handful of medical marijuana studies have been allowed to proceed, and only one is presently under way. These have been small pilot studies, and while they have been consistently successful, the federal government is actively obstructing the type of medical marijuana studies that would be needed to obtain FDA approval. Most notably, a group of researchers at the University of Massachusetts at Amherst has been seeking to conduct formal trials for years, but the Drug Enforcement Administration is blocking their efforts. The researchers are trying to create a facility to grow specific marijuana strains under controlled, reproducible conditions to test marijuana's efficacy for various indications. Such research is essential for FDA approval, but the DEA has refused to approve such a facility.

Vaporizers allow patients to inhale cannabinoid vapors without smoking.

What Research Has Shown

Objection: There haven't been any double-blind, placebo-controlled studies proving marijuana's effectiveness.

Reply: Despite the many difficulties in acquiring marijuana for research, in 2007, Dr. Donald Abrams of the University of California, San Francisco [UCSF], published just such a study that found marijuana to be safe and effective at treating peripheral neuropathy, which causes great suffering to HIV/AIDS patients. There are no FDA-approved treatments for peripheral neuropathy, which is notoriously resistant to treatment with conventional pain medications. In the UCSF study, marijuana was clearly shown to give relief. In this randomized, double-blind, placebo-controlled trial, a majority of patients had a greater than 30 percent reduction in pain after smoking marijuana. In another randomized, double-blind, placebo-controlled study published in April 2008 by the *Journal of Pain*, marijuana was found to be effective at relieving neuropathic pain from a variety of causes, including diabetes, multiple sclerosis, and spinal injury.

Objection: There has been no research on nonsmoked delivery systems for marijuana.

Reply: The IOM expressed concern about the health risks of smoking and urged development of a "nonsmoked, rapid-onset cannabinoid drug delivery system," but noted that in the meantime, "we acknowledge that there is no clear alternative for people suffering from chronic conditions that might be relieved by smoking marijuana, such as pain or AIDS wasting." The answer to the IOM's concerns about smoking is vaporizers, which take advantage of the fact that cannabinoids vaporize at a temperature well below that at which marijuana burns. Vaporizers allow patients to inhale cannabinoid vapors without smoking, achieving the same rapid action and easy dose titration without the tars and other irritants found in smoke. Several studies of such devices have now been published. In a study of one such device, the Volcano, researchers confirmed that the device works as intended, stating, "What is currently needed for optimal use of medicinal cannabinoids is a feasible, nonsmoked, rapid-onset delivery system. With the Volcano, a safe and effective delivery system appears to be available to patients."

Objection: Sativex will be approved soon.

Reply: Sativex is a concentrated extract of the components of natural marijuana that has been developed for sublingual use to counter pain associated with advanced cancer and pain/ spasticity associated with multiple sclerosis. An FDA-approved clinical study for advanced cancer pain is under way. Additional studies will likely be needed prior to approval by the

FDA, making it likely that Sativex would not be available in the U.S. for at least three more years. Meanwhile, many thousands of people are already obtaining significant symptom relief with medical marijuana in the 13 states with medical marijuana programs, but they are still subject to federal prosecution and intimidation. Sativex may well prove to be a useful product, but it has been shown to have drawbacks. It takes far longer to reach peak blood levels than inhaled marijuana, and the alcohol-based spray has been associated with oral lesions.

Research Shows That Marijuana Is Not Dangerous

Russ Belville

Russ Belville produces the National Organization for the Reform of Marijuana Laws' (NORML's) blog, The NORML Stash, *and hosts NORML's streaming talk radio show* NORML SHOW LIVE: Marijuana Nation.

If Dr. Sanjay Gupta is picked for the post of surgeon general, he would become the nation's leading medical advocate. His experience in the media would be beneficial in bringing the surgeon general's office back to the prominence it held when [former surgeon general] C. Everett Koop was successfully battling tobacco smoking.

Gupta's Outrageous Claims

But is Gupta ready to deliver the [Barack] Obama administration's promised end to the politicization of science and medicine? More specifically, will Gupta toe the federal line that cannabis is lacking in any medical value, or will he recognize what 13 states and the past 12 years of research prove—that cannabis is a beneficial medicine for some people and an intoxicant far less harmful than alcohol for others?

In 2002, Gupta was more than willing to echo the outrageous claims that smoking pot would lead to psychosis, depression and schizophrenia:

> But the three studies you are talking about talk specifically about schizophrenia and depression, and the fact that marijuana use earlier in life actually may lead to an increased—30 percent increase—in schizophrenia later in life.
>
> Depression, also a very big diagnosis—roughly 18.8 million in this country have it. Again, they looked this time at 1,600

Russ Belville, "Sanjay Gupta: What the Next Surgeon General Doesn't Know About Pot," *AlterNet*, January 8, 2009. www.alternet.org. Reproduced by permission of NORML.

high school students and followed them over about seven years. This is in Australia, not in the United States. But they actually found that all of these boys and girls, particularly girls, were more vulnerable to the symptoms of depression later on in life, again if they were frequent or even daily marijuana users.

The Research on Marijuana

I hope that the next surgeon general has been following the research on cannabis and mental health since 2002. This year [2009], Dr. Mikkel Arendt of Aarhus University in Risskov, Denmark, said that people treated for a so-called cannabis-induced psychosis " . . . would have developed schizophrenia whether or not they used cannabis."

I hope that Gupta has kept up with the journal *Schizophrenia Research* and the research published there last year by London's Institute of Psychiatry, which found no statistically significant "differences in symptomatology between schizophrenic patients who were or were not cannabis users," found no "evidence that cannabis users with schizophrenia were more likely to have a family member with the disorder" and that these findings "argue against a distinct schizophrenic-like psychosis caused by cannabis," authors concluded.

Regarding depression, in 2006, researchers at Johns Hopkins University's Bloomberg School of Public Health in Baltimore found "that the associations observed between marijuana use and subsequent depression status may be attributable not to continued marijuana use, per se, but to third (common) factors associated with both the decision to use marijuana and to depression." In fact, the year prior, researchers at USC [University of Southern California] had found among cannabis smokers, "those who used once per week or less had less depressed mood, more positive affect and fewer somatic (physical) complaints than nonusers," and that "[d]aily users [also] reported less depressed mood and more positive affect than nonusers."

Or we could just ask the incoming surgeon general to apply some common sense. If smoking cannabis is a strong predictor of future depression or schizophrenia, then shouldn't there be a spike in the reporting of those conditions around 1978, when 37 percent of high school seniors reported past-month cannabis use, and a decline in depression and schizophrenia around 1992, when the modern low of 12 percent was reported? Instead, what we find is that about 1 percent of the population develops schizophrenia, and that figure stays relatively steady even as cannabis use rises and falls.

The Government's Antidrug Propaganda

In 2006, Gupta was penning the article "Why I Would Vote No on Pot" for *Time* magazine as Colorado and Nevada had nonmedical-cannabis-regulation ballot measures pending. It doesn't seem like he's been following the past two decades of research:

> I'm constantly amazed that after all these years—and all the wars on drugs and all the public service announcements [PSAs]—nearly 15 million Americans still use marijuana at least once a month.
>
> Frequent marijuana use can seriously affect your short-term memory. It can impair your cognitive ability (why do you think people call it dope?) and lead to long-lasting depression or anxiety. While many people smoke marijuana to relax, it can have the opposite effect on frequent users. And smoking anything, whether it's tobacco or marijuana, can seriously damage your lung tissue.
>
> But I'm here to tell you, as a doctor, that despite all the talk about the medical benefits of marijuana, smoking the stuff is not going to do your health any good. And if you get high before climbing behind the wheel of a car, you will be putting yourself and those around you in danger.

First, I'm wondering what Gupta is amazed about—that 15 million Americans trust their own experiences with cannabis over government antidrug propaganda and hyperbole? The antidrug PSAs he mentions have been proven to not reduce teen cannabis use and may actually increase it. The Annenberg Public Policy Center of the University of Pennsylvania was commissioned by the National Institute on Drug Abuse to study the effect of government anti-cannabis ad campaigns over four years and found, "Youth who were more exposed to campaign messages are no more likely to hold favorable beliefs or intentions about marijuana than are youth less exposed to those messages, both during the marijuana initiative period and over the entire course of the campaign."

All the pulmonary harms of smoking cannabis can be alleviated through eating it or through cannabis vaporization.

Gupta claims that smoking cannabis will impair your cognitive ability, and again, I fear he's parroting politics rather than following the research. Just this November, the journal *Neuropsychopharmacology* published data from Columbia University that reported "the finding that accuracy [on cognitive testing] was unaffected by smoked marijuana indicates that heavy, daily marijuana smokers will not fulfill the DSM-IV [*Diagnostic and Statistical Manual of Mental Disorders*, 4th edition] criterion for marijuana intoxication that requires impairment of complex cognitive functioning." This is on the heels of a Harvard study published in the *Archives of General Psychiatry* that determined that long-term marijuana smokers who abstain from the drug for one week or more perform identically on cognition tests as nonusers, and a previous study on marijuana and cognition by researchers at Johns Hopkins that found "no significant differences in cognitive decline between heavy users, light users and nonusers of cannabis" over a 15-year period in a cohort of 1,318 subjects.

The Alleged Harms of Smoking Marijuana

Gupta also makes the mistake of comparing tobacco smoke to cannabis smoke. While it is true that long-term cannabis smoking can lead to wheezing, cough and bronchitis, investigators writing last year in the journal *Thorax* did not find a positive association between smoking cannabis and the development of emphysema (overinflation of the air sacs in the lungs). Of course, all the pulmonary harms of smoking cannabis can be alleviated through eating it or through cannabis vaporization. Investigators at San Francisco General Hospital reported last year in the journal *Clinical Pharmacology & Therapeutics* that the "vaporization of marijuana does not result in exposure to combustion gases." A previous clinical trial, published in 2006 in the *Journal of Pharmaceutical Sciences*, reported that vaporization is a "safe and effective" cannabinoid delivery system that "avoid[s] the respiratory disadvantages of smoking."

In 1997, Dr. Donald Tashkin's research at the UCLA [University of California, Los Angeles] Medical Center found that, "Neither the continuing nor the intermittent marijuana smokers exhibited any significantly different rates of decline in [lung function]" as compared with those individuals who never smoked marijuana. "No differences were noted between even quite heavy marijuana smoking and nonsmoking of marijuana." These findings starkly contrasted those experienced by tobacco-only smokers who suffered a significant rate of decline in lung function.

By 2006, the *Washington Post* reported on Tashkin's latest research on cannabis use and cancer. Tashkin said, "We hypothesized that there would be a positive association between marijuana use and lung cancer, and that the association would be more positive with heavier use. What we found instead was no association at all, and even a suggestion of some protective effect."

As for driving, nobody here at NORML [National Organization for the Reform of Marijuana Laws] suggests that people smoke cannabis and then drive a car. But someone's potential irresponsible use of cannabis is not an argument for the danger of cannabis itself. In fact, researchers at Britain's Transport Research Laboratory found in September [2008] that text messaging and alcohol are far more dangerous on the road than cannabis. "The reaction times of people texting as they drove fell by 35 percent, while those who had consumed the legal limit of alcohol, or taken cannabis, fell by 21 percent and 12 percent respectively."

The Medicine of Last Resort

To be fair, in his 2006 *Time* article, Gupta does seem to begrudgingly admit some of cannabis's vast medicinal uses:

> Several recent studies, including a new one from the Scripps Research Institute, show that THC [tetrahydrocannabinol], the chemical in marijuana responsible for the high, can help slow the progress of Alzheimer's disease. (In fact, it seems to block the formation of disease-causing plaques better than several mainstream drugs.) Other studies have shown THC to be a very effective antinausea treatment for people—cancer patients undergoing chemotherapy, for example—for whom conventional medications aren't working. And medical cannabis has shown promise relieving pain in patients with multiple sclerosis and reducing intraocular pressure in glaucoma patients.

But back in 2002, even when he gives in on the most recognized medical uses of cannabis, he still recites the government line that there are other drugs that can be used instead of cannabis:

> There are some benefits to marijuana use. It can make cancer chemotherapy patients hungrier—also in HIV and AIDS patients. . . . And marijuana can offer some of those things,

especially when it comes to reducing nausea and vomiting, not advocating that necessarily myself. I think there are other ways to do that besides marijuana.

This is the mind-set I call "marijuana as medicine of last resort." It's the concept that any time a medical benefit to cannabis is absolutely undeniable, then it can be somewhat accepted, but only if no other medicine will suffice. This "medicine of last resort" idea is the notion that if both OxyContin and cannabis will relieve pain, you should take OxyContin because it is legal, despite the fact that OxyContin is addictive and has severe side effects. It's the notion that if you're vomiting from severe nausea, you should first try to swallow a synthetic THC pill called Marinol that won't work for 45 minutes rather than smoking an illegal doobie that works immediately. Even when cannabis is the *superior* medicine for a symptom or condition, the drug-war mentality that there are "good" drugs and "bad" drugs kicks in, and the doctors will recommend a less-effective "good" drug over the more-effective "bad" one.

Even when cannabis is the superior *medicine for a symptom or condition, the drug-war mentality that there are "good" drugs and "bad" drugs kicks in.*

The Inconvenient Truths About Marijuana

In a weekly radio address to the nation, President-elect Barack Obama offered his view of science and public policy:

> Because the truth is that promoting science isn't just about providing resources—it's about protecting free and open inquiry. It's about ensuring that facts and evidence are never twisted or obscured by politics or ideology. It's about listening to what our scientists have to say, even when it's inconvenient—especially when it's inconvenient. Because the highest purpose of science is the search for knowledge, truth and

a greater understanding of the world around us. That will be my goal as president of the United States—and I could not have a better team to guide me in this work.

If your team is going to ensure the science behind medical cannabis isn't twisted by ideology, we'd invite you and Gupta to meet with us here at NORML so we can show you all the inconvenient truths about cannabis that have been discovered over the past 12 years. Thirteen states and millions of medical users are depending on you to support the truth, not the politics, Dr. Gupta. Will you have the courage of another surgeon general, Dr. Joycelyn Elders, who testified in support of medical marijuana in Rhode Island, saying:

> The evidence is overwhelming that marijuana can relieve certain types of pain, nausea, vomiting and other symptoms caused by such illnesses as multiple sclerosis, cancer and AIDS—or by the harsh drugs sometimes used to treat them. And it can do so with remarkable safety. Indeed, marijuana is less toxic than many of the drugs that physicians prescribe every day. It is simply wrong for the sick and suffering to be casualties in the war on drugs. Let's get rid of the myths and institute sound public health policy.

Sound public health policy free from drug-war mythology? President-elect Obama, Dr. Gupta, *that* is the kind of change we can believe in. [Gupta withdrew his name from consideration for surgeon general in March 2009.]

CHAPTER 3

Should Marijuana Use Be Regulated by the Government?

Overview: American Opinion on Marijuana Regulation

Gary Langer

Gary Langer provides public opinion polling, analysis, and consulting services through Langer Research Associates to ABC News and other media outlets.

Eight in 10 Americans support legalizing marijuana for medical use and nearly half favor decriminalizing the drug more generally, both far higher than a decade ago.

Public Opinion on Marijuana

With New Jersey this week poised to become the 14th state to legalize medical marijuana [signed into law on January 19, 2010], 81 percent in this national ABC News/*Washington Post* poll support the idea, up from an already substantial 69 percent in 1997. Indeed the main complaint is with restrictions on access, as in the New Jersey law.

Fifty-six percent say that if it's allowed, doctors should be able to prescribe medical marijuana to anyone they think it can help. New Jersey's measure, which is more restrictive than most, limits prescriptions to people with severe illnesses. State health officials can add to the list.

Apart from medical marijuana, there have been recent efforts to decriminalize marijuana more broadly in some states. A preliminary vote on one such measure is to be held in the Washington State legislature this week [the decriminalization proposal was rejected]. In California organizers say they've collected enough signatures to hold a statewide referendum on the issue next fall. And a separate proposal in California to legalize and tax the drug cleared a legislative committee last

Gary Langer, "High Support for Medical Marijuana," *ABC News*, January 18, 2010. Reproduced by permission.

week. A Field poll there in April [2009] found 56 percent support for the idea, which its backers say would raise $1.3 billion a year.

Nationally, this survey finds 46 percent support for legalizing small amounts of marijuana for personal use—the same as it was last spring, and well above its level in past years, for example 39 percent in 2002 and 22 percent in 1997.

The Demographics of Opinion

Age is a factor. Just 23 percent of senior citizens favor legalizing marijuana for personal use; that jumps to 51 percent of adults under age 65. There are political and ideological differences as well: Thirty percent of conservatives and 32 percent of Republicans favor legalization, compared with 49 percent of independents, 53 percent of Democrats and more than half of moderates and liberals alike (53 and 63 percent, respectively).

Medical marijuana, for its part, receives majority support across the political and ideological spectrum, from 68 percent of conservatives and 72 percent of Republicans as well as 85 percent of Democrats and independents and about nine in 10 liberals and moderates. Support slips to 69 percent among seniors, vs. 83 percent among all adults under age 65.

There are similar divisions on whether medical marijuana should be restricted or made available to anyone a doctor thinks it would help. Overall, 56 percent, as noted, prefer no restrictions, while 21 percent say it should be limited to terminally ill patients and an additional 21 percent say it should be limited to those with serious but not necessarily terminal illnesses.

Liberals are 23 points more apt than conservatives, and Democrats 20 points more likely than Republicans, to oppose restrictions. There's also a difference between the sexes, with men 10 points more likely than women to say the doctor should decide.

Marijuana for Medical Use

But the main difference is whether people think marijuana should be permitted for medical uses in the first place. Among supporters, 63 percent would rely on the doctor's discretion. Among those who oppose medical marijuana, 75 percent say that if it is allowed, it should be limited to seriously or terminally ill patients.

New Jersey passed its medical marijuana law this month and outgoing Gov. Jon Corzine is expected to sign it tomorrow morning, his last day in office. Medical marijuana first became legal in California in 1996, followed by Alaska, Colorado, Hawaii, Maine, Michigan, Montana, Nevada, New Mexico, Oregon, Rhode Island, Vermont and Washington State.

Congress Should Lift Legal Restrictions on Medical Marijuana

Marijuana Policy Project

The Marijuana Policy Project is an organization working to reform marijuana laws by legalizing medical marijuana and eliminating criminal penalties for all marijuana use.

For thousands of years, marijuana has been used to treat a wide variety of ailments. Until 1937, marijuana (*Cannabis sativa L*) was legal in the United States for all purposes. Presently, federal law allows only four Americans to use marijuana as a medicine.

On March 17, 1999, the National Academy of Sciences' Institute of Medicine (IOM) concluded that "there are some limited circumstances in which we recommend smoking marijuana for medical uses." The IOM report, the result of two years of research that was funded by the White House drug policy office, analyzed all existing data on marijuana's therapeutic uses.

The Medical Value of Marijuana

Marijuana is one of the safest therapeutically active substances known. No one has ever died from an overdose, and it has a wide variety of therapeutic applications, including:

- Relief from nausea and appetite loss;

- Reduction of intraocular (within the eye) pressure;

- Reduction of muscle spasms; and

- Relief from chronic pain.

Marijuana Policy Project, "Medical Marijuana Briefing Paper: The Need to Change State and Federal Law," January 2010. www.mpp.org. Reproduced by permission.

Marijuana is frequently beneficial in the treatment of the following conditions:

AIDS. Marijuana can reduce the nausea, vomiting, and loss of appetite caused by the ailment itself and by various AIDS medications. Observational research has found that by relieving these side effects, medical marijuana increases the ability of patients to stay on life-extending treatment.

Hepatitis C. As with AIDS, marijuana can relieve the nausea and vomiting caused by treatments for hepatitis C. In a study published in the September 2006 *European Journal of Gastroenterology & Hepatology*, patients using marijuana were better able to complete their medication regimens, leading to a 300% improvement in treatment success.

Glaucoma. Marijuana can reduce intraocular pressure, alleviating the pain and slowing—and sometimes stopping—damage to the eyes. (Glaucoma is the leading cause of blindness in the United States. It damages vision by increasing eye pressure over time.)

Cancer. Marijuana can stimulate the appetite and alleviate nausea and vomiting, which are common side effects of chemotherapy treatment.

Multiple Sclerosis. Marijuana can limit the muscle pain and spasticity caused by the disease, as well as relieve tremor and unsteadiness of gait. (Multiple sclerosis is the leading cause of neurological disability among young and middle-aged adults in the United States.)

Marijuana could be helpful for millions of patients in the United States.

Epilepsy. Marijuana can prevent epileptic seizures in some patients.

Chronic Pain. Marijuana can alleviate chronic, often debilitating pain caused by myriad disorders and injuries. Since 2007, three published clinical trials have found that marijuana effectively relieves neuropathic pain (pain caused by nerve injury), a particularly hard to treat type of pain that afflicts millions suffering from diabetes, HIV/AIDS, multiple sclerosis, and other illnesses.

Each of these applications has been deemed legitimate by at least one court, legislature, and/or government agency in the United States.

Many patients also report that marijuana is useful for treating arthritis, migraine, menstrual cramps, alcohol and opiate addiction, and depression and other debilitating mood disorders.

Marijuana could be helpful for millions of patients in the United States. Nevertheless, other than for the four people with special permission from the federal government, medical marijuana remains illegal under federal law!

People currently suffering from any of the conditions mentioned above, for whom the legal medical options have proven unsafe or ineffective, have two options:

1. Continue to suffer without effective treatment; or

2. Illegally obtain marijuana—and risk suffering consequences directly related to its illegality, such as:

- an insufficient supply due to the prohibition-inflated price or scarcity; impure, contaminated, or chemically adulterated marijuana;

- arrests, fines, court costs, property forfeiture, incarceration, probation, and criminal records.

The Background of Federal Marijuana Law

Prior to 1937, at least 27 medicines containing marijuana were legally available in the United States. Many were made by well-known pharmaceutical firms that still exist today, such as Squibb (now Bristol-Myers Squibb) and Eli Lilly. The Marihuana Tax Act of 1937 federally prohibited marijuana. Dr. William C. Woodward of the American Medical Association opposed the act, testifying that prohibition would ultimately prevent the medical uses of marijuana.

The Controlled Substances Act of 1970 placed all illicit and prescription drugs into five "schedules" (categories). Marijuana was placed in Schedule I, defining it as having a high potential for abuse, no currently accepted medical use in treatment in the United States, and a lack of accepted safety for use under medical supervision.

This definition simply does not apply to marijuana. Of course, at the time of the Controlled Substances Act, marijuana had been prohibited for more than three decades. Its medical uses forgotten, marijuana was considered a dangerous and addictive narcotic.

A substantial increase in the number of recreational users in the 1970s contributed to the rediscovery of marijuana's medical uses:

- Many scientists studied the health effects of marijuana and inadvertently discovered marijuana's medical uses in the process.

- Many who used marijuana recreationally also suffered from diseases for which marijuana is beneficial. By accident, they discovered its therapeutic value.

As the word spread, more and more patients started self-medicating with marijuana. However, marijuana's Schedule I status bars doctors from prescribing it and severely curtails research.

The Struggle in Court

In 1972, a petition was submitted to the Bureau of Narcotics and Dangerous Drugs—now the Drug Enforcement Administration (DEA)—to reschedule marijuana to make it available by prescription.

After 16 years of court battles, the DEA's chief administrative law judge, Francis L. Young, ruled on September 6, 1988:

"Marijuana, in its natural form, is one of the safest therapeutically active substances known. . . . "

" . . . [T]he provisions of the [Controlled Substances] Act permit and require the transfer of marijuana from Schedule I to Schedule II."

"It would be unreasonable, arbitrary and capricious for DEA to continue to stand between those sufferers and the benefits of this substance. . . . "

Marijuana's placement in Schedule II would enable doctors to prescribe it to their patients. But top DEA bureaucrats rejected Judge Young's ruling and refused to reschedule marijuana. Two appeals later, petitioners experienced their first defeat in the 22-year-old lawsuit. On February 18, 1994, the U.S. Court of Appeals (D.C. Circuit) ruled that the DEA is allowed to reject its judge's ruling and set its own criteria—enabling the DEA to keep marijuana in Schedule I.

However, Congress has the power to reschedule marijuana via legislation, regardless of the DEA's wishes.

There is wide support for ending the prohibition of medical marijuana among both the public and the medical community.

The Compassionate Access Program

In 1975, Robert Randall, who suffered from glaucoma, was arrested for cultivating his own marijuana. He won his case by using the "medical necessity defense," forcing the government to find a way to provide him with his medicine. As a result, the Investigational New Drug (IND) compassionate access program was established, enabling some patients to receive marijuana from the government.

The program was grossly inadequate at helping the potentially millions of people who need medical marijuana. Many patients would never consider the idea that an illegal drug might be their best medicine, and most who were fortunate enough to discover marijuana's medical value did not discover the IND program. Those who did often could not find doctors willing to take on the program's arduous, bureaucratic requirements.

In 1992, in response to a flood of new applications from AIDS patients, the George H.W. Bush administration closed the program to new applicants, and pleas to reopen it were ignored by subsequent administrations. The IND program remains in operation only for the four surviving, previously approved patients.

Public and Professional Opinion

There is wide support for ending the prohibition of medical marijuana among both the public and the medical community:

• Since 1996, a majority of voters in Alaska, California, Colorado, the District of Columbia, Maine, Michigan, Montana, Nevada, Oregon, and Washington State have voted in favor of ballot initiatives to remove criminal penalties for seriously ill people who grow or possess medical marijuana.

• A national ABC News/*Washington Post* poll released January 18, 2010, found that 81% of Americans "think doctors should be allowed to prescribe marijuana for medical purposes to treat their patients." That figure is up from 69% in 1997. A national Gallup poll released November 1, 2005, found that 78% of Americans support "making marijuana legally available for doctors to prescribe in order to reduce pain and suffering." Polls conducted in the 11 states with medical marijuana laws during 2006 found support for the laws was high and steady, or (in nearly all cases) increasing.

• Organizations supporting some form of physician-supervised access to medical marijuana include the American Academy of Family Physicians, American Nurses Association,

American Public Health Association, American Academy of HIV Medicine, and many others.

• A 1990 scientific survey of oncologists (cancer specialists) found that 54% of those with an opinion favored the controlled medical availability of marijuana and 44% had already suggested at least once that a patient obtain marijuana illegally.

The federal government has no legal authority to prevent state governments from changing their laws to remove state-level penalties for medical marijuana use. Fourteen states have already done so: Hawaii, Rhode Island, New Jersey, New Mexico, and Vermont through their legislatures and the others by ballot initiatives. State legislatures have the authority and moral responsibility to change state law to:

- exempt seriously ill patients from state-level prosecution for medical marijuana possession and cultivation; and

- exempt doctors who recommend medical marijuana from prosecution or the denial of any right or privilege.

Even within the confines of federal law, states can enact reforms that have the practical effect of removing the fear of patients being arrested and prosecuted under state law—as well as the symbolic effect of pushing the federal government to allow doctors to prescribe marijuana.

Congress has the power and the responsibility to change federal law so that seriously ill people nationwide can use medical marijuana.

The Need to Change Federal Law

State governments that want to allow marijuana to be sold in pharmacies have been stymied by the federal government's overriding prohibition of marijuana.

The U.S. Supreme Court's June 2005 decision in *Gonzales v. Raich* preserved state medical marijuana laws but allowed continued federal attacks on patients, even in states with such laws. While the Justice Department indicated in 2009 that it would refrain from raids where activity is clearly legal under state law, that policy change could be reversed anytime.

Efforts to obtain FDA [Food and Drug Administration] approval of marijuana also remain stalled. Though some small studies of marijuana have been published or are under way, the National Institute on Drug Abuse—the only legal source of marijuana for clinical research in the U.S.—has consistently made it difficult (and often nearly impossible) for researchers to obtain marijuana for their studies. At present, it is effectively impossible to do the sort of large-scale, extremely costly trials required for FDA approval.

In the meantime, patients continue to suffer. Congress has the power and the responsibility to change federal law so that seriously ill people nationwide can use medical marijuana without fear of arrest and imprisonment.

Marijuana Should Be Regulated Like Other Prescription Medicines

Paul Armentano

Paul Armentano is the deputy director of the National Organization for the Reform of Marijuana Laws (NORML) and the NORML Foundation.

Ten years ago today [March 17, 2009], the use of medical marijuana went from fringe to mainstream.

The Mainstreaming of Medical Marijuana

March 17, 2009, marks the 10-year anniversary of the publication of the Institute of Medicine's landmark study on medical cannabis: *Marijuana and Medicine: Assessing the Science Base.* At the time this report was commissioned, in response to the passage of California's Compassionate Use Act of 1996 [Proposition 215], many in the public and the mainstream media were skeptical about pot's potential therapeutic value. The publication of the Institute of Medicine's findings—which concluded that marijuana possessed medicinal properties to treat and control pain and to stimulate appetite—provided the issue with long-overdue credibility, and began in earnest a political discourse that continues today.

Of course, much has changed over the past 10 years. For starters, a total of 13 states, encompassing some 72 million Americans, now allow for the medical use of cannabis under state law. In California, several clinical trials have been conducted over the past months demonstrating that inhaled cannabis can significantly reduce hard-to-treat neuropathic pain in patients with HIV and spinal cord injury.

Paul Armentano, "Medical Marijuana Has Come of Age: Celebrating the 10th Anniversary of a Landmark Scientific Study," Reason.com, March 17, 2009. Reproduced by permission.

A Growth in Marijuana Research

Following the publication of the Institute of Medicine's report, scientific interest into the therapeutic properties of cannabis skyrocketed. A key word search using the terms "cannabis, 1999" in the National Library of Medicine's PubMed website reveals just 427 scientific journal articles published on the subject during that year. Perform this same search for the year 2008, and one will find over 2,100 published scientific studies.

Whereas researchers in the 1970s, 80s, and 90s primarily assessed cannabis's ability to temporarily alleviate various disease symptoms, scientists today are exploring the potential role of medical marijuana to treat disease itself.

Of particular interest, scientists are investigating marijuana's capacity to moderate autoimmune disorders such as multiple sclerosis, rheumatoid arthritis, and inflammatory bowel disease, as well as its role in the treatment of neurological disorders such as Alzheimer's disease and Lou Gehrig's disease.

Investigators are also studying the anti-cancer activities of cannabis, which has been shown to halt malignant tumor growth in animals. Arguably, these later trends represent far broader and more significant applications for cannabinoid therapeutics than the Institute of Medicine's researchers could have imagined just 10 years ago.

Medical Marijuana Delivery Systems

We've also discovered alternative ways to safely, effectively, and rapidly deliver pot's therapeutic properties to patients. Writing in 1999, the Institute of Medicine concluded, "Except for the harms associated with smoking, the adverse effects of marijuana are within the range of effects tolerated for other medications." The authors went on to recommend the development of "rapid-onset cannabinoid [marijuana] formulations."

Today, such rapid-onset delivery systems exist in the form of vaporizers, devices which heat cannabis to a temperature where active vapors form but below the point of combustion where noxious smoke and associated toxins are produced. In 2007, investigators at San Francisco General Hospital assessed this technology and concluded: "Vaporization of marijuana does not result in exposure to combustion gasses ... and [was] preferred by most subjects compared to marijuana cigarettes. The [vaporizer] device is an effective and apparently safe vehicle for THC delivery."

Lessons Learned

As hundreds of thousands of Americans have begun using marijuana under their doctors' supervision, we've learned other lessons as well. First, we've affirmed that medical cannabis is remarkably safe. For example, in 2008 investigators at McGill University in Montreal reviewed over 30 years of data on marijuana and "did not find a higher incidence rate of serious adverse events associated with medical cannabis use" compared to those who never used the drug.

The use of medical cannabis is here to stay.

We've also discovered that restricted patient access to medicinal cannabis will not necessarily result in higher use rates among young people. In fact, since the passage of Proposition 215, the use of pot by young people has fallen at a greater rate than the national average.

And finally we've learned—much to the chagrin of our opponents—that in fact the sky will not fall. Rates of hard drug use and drugged driving have not increased in California, and our social value system has not "gone to pot."

So what can we expect over the next 10 years? Only time will tell, but one thing is certain: The use of medical cannabis is here to stay. It is time for our federal laws to reflect this reality, and it is time for our politicians to regulate marijuana like other accepted prescription medicines.

The Time Is Right to Abolish Federal Prohibition of Marijuana

Mike Miliard

Mike Miliard is managing editor for Healthcare IT News *and a frequent contributing writer for the* Phoenix, *an alternative newsweekly based in Boston.*

The [Barack] Obama administration, already overtaxed with two foreign campaigns, made headlines this past week when it waved a white flag in a fight much closer to home. [On May 11, 2009] Gil Kerlikowske, the White House's newly minted director of the Office of National Drug Control Policy—the so-called drug czar—called for an end to the "War on Drugs."

Granted, Kerlikowske wasn't signaling an intention to lay down arms and pick up a pack of E-Z Wider [rolling papers]. His was a semantic shift—a pledge to abandon gung-ho fighting words and imprisonment in favor of treatment. But it was newsworthy nonetheless. As Bruce Mirken, communications director of the Marijuana Policy Project—the biggest pot-policy-reform group in the country—puts it: "Can you imagine [Bush administration drug czar] John Walters saying that? The earth would open up!"

It wouldn't be surprising if Kerlikowske's speech was actually a subtle testing of the political landscape surrounding the marijuana question, as we find ourselves, quite suddenly, at a pivotal moment in the push for pot legalization.

The Trend Toward Marijuana Reform

The horrific violence of Mexican cartels, which make perhaps as much as 75 percent of their money from marijuana (in

Mike Miliard, "Legalize Pot Now," *The Phoenix* (Boston, MA), June 1, 2009. www.the phoenix.com. Reproduced by permission.

Arizona attorney general Terry Goddard's estimation), has started ebbing across our Southwestern borders. The budget meltdown in California has led state pols [politicians]—even, once unthinkably, GOP [Republican] governor Arnold Schwarzenegger—to reconsider the tax revenues ($14 billion, according to *Time*) that could be harvested from the Golden State's biggest cash crop. Politicians, no longer confined to the left and libertarian right, are increasingly willing to say that legalization makes sense.

Nearly every day offers another object lesson in the merits of marijuana reform. And the American people seem to be noticing. At least four polls in the past three months have shown a greater uptick in the public's receptiveness to legalization than ever before. One Zogby poll released earlier this month found that 52 percent felt pot should be regulated and taxed. Among the more than 13,000 questions submitted to President Barack Obama's online town hall in March, the *Los Angeles Times* reported, the top six questions in the "budget" category had to do with legalizing and taxing pot (thanks in part to prodding from groups such as NORML, the National Organization for the Reform of Marijuana Laws).

So far, the president—who supported decriminalization when running for Senate in 2004, but not when running for president in 2008—hasn't exactly been a profile in courage. (His answer, at that town hall, to the question of taxing marijuana was wincingly flippant.) But that may not matter all that much. "Obama is against gay marriage, at least nominally, yet that issue is moving forward, too," statistician Nate Silver, founder of Fivethirtyeight.com, tells the *Phoenix*. "Once one state does something, then other states start to think about it."

Even if Obama isn't yet bumping *Pineapple Express* [a comedy about marijuana] to the top of his Netflix queue, then, this much seems clear: the thoughtfulness he's brought to Washington—zealots out, pragmatists in—is evident. And suddenly, whether his fingerprints are on it directly or not, "change" may be more than just a buzzword.

As seen in a steady spate of headlines over the past six months, we're talking about the failed drug war and the ever-widening patchwork of individual state laws with a measure of honesty and common sense that's not been heard since the 1970s.

None of which is to say the trend is inexorable. But this may be the moment. If we don't see an end to marijuana prohibition in the next decade or so, it's reasonable to say that there's a fair chance it'll never happen. And that, as some are wont to say, would be an enormous harshing of one's mellow.

The Pendulum of Public Opinion

In the '70s, as a member of the Massachusetts House of Representatives, Barney Frank filed a bill that sought to allow possession and use of small amounts of marijuana. It went nowhere.

Then last April, as a US congressman, he co-sponsored, with Ron Paul, the Personal Use of Marijuana by Responsible Adults Act of 2008, which would have lifted federal penalties for possessing 3.5 ounces or less. That bill never made it to committee. This past month, though, Frank and Paul introduced another bill that *did* reach the committee stage, the Industrial Hemp Farming Act of 2009, which would end the ban on cultivation of non-psychoactive hemp.

"I think people have gotten more skeptical of government intervention," says Frank. "And I think people have seen the ineffectiveness of the all-out-war approach to all this. Third, we have concerns about the costs, about overcrowded prisons and overstretched law enforcement. So I think things are moving. But the basic thing is that Americans are better understanding now of personal freedoms."

"A lot of things are being put on the table that people couldn't imagine until just recently," says Ethan Nadelmann, founder and executive director of the Drug Policy Alliance, which seeks an end to the worldwide war on drugs. "I would not have predicted five months ago that we'd have this explosion of sentiment. I'm stunned."

Mirken, too, is cautiously optimistic that we may be laying the groundwork for substantial progress. "We'll know for sure five years from now," he says. "But there's certainly much more intense interest in and discussion of whether our marijuana laws make any sense than I've seen since I was a kid— *i.e.*[that is], when [Richard] Nixon was president."

Indeed, back in the heyday of Cheech and Chong [referring to the comedy duo consisting of Richard "Cheech" Marin and Tommy Chong], the prospects for legalization looked promising. "There were a bunch of states that passed decriminalization statutes in the '70s," says Mirken, including New York, Colorado, and even Mississippi.

More than 40 percent of Americans have tried marijuana.

"Then basically everything ground to a halt in the [President Ronald] Reagan era. The pendulum had swung in one direction in the '60s and '70s and then swung back."

It may have swung back yet again—perhaps for good this time. "Back then [in the '70s, pro-legalization] public opinion never topped more than 30 percent," says Nadelmann. "And there was a whole generation that didn't know the difference between marijuana and heroin. Now, support is topping 30 percent nationally."

"We're not yet there, but look at the number of states who voted for medical marijuana," says Frank. "Then you had the referendum in Massachusetts last year over the objection of almost all law enforcement people. There is movement."

The Economic Impact of Legalization

Rock Band [a video game] enthusiasts with bongs aren't the only ones taking note. More than 40 percent of Americans have tried marijuana, according to the National Institute on Drug Abuse. By NORML's tally, as many as 15 million people smoke at least once a month. That's a pretty substantial market, and one that could bring in a goodly amount of tax revenue—a fact that hasn't been lost on those seeking rational solutions to our nation's financial woes.

"When you're staring at the sort of budget deficits that governments at all levels are looking at right now, that clarifies the mind a great deal," says Mirken. "And it does, I think, begin to strike people as pretty absurd that we have this huge industry that is effectively tax exempt!"

California assemblyman Tom Ammiano made news in February when he introduced a bill that would essentially treat pot like alcohol: legalize it, tax it, and allow adults 21 and over to purchase and use it. Soon after, the state's Board of Equalization announced that the bill's proposed levy of $50 per ounce could put as much as $1.3 billion a year into government coffers.

"I think it's not time for that," Schwarzenegger said in response. "But I think it's time for a debate."

"He's far and away the highest-placed politician in recent memory who's dared to broach the subject at all," says Harvard economist Jeffrey Miron of Schwarzenegger. "He said, 'I'm not in favor of it, but let's discuss it.' Well, why are you gonna discuss it when you're so sure it's a bad idea? He clearly does think it might be a good idea."

Miron is the author of a 2005 study titled *The Budgetary Implications of Marijuana Prohibition.* In it, he looks at the money that could be saved by local, state, and federal governments by the cessation of prohibition, and that could be gained by taxing pot at rates comparable with those levied on other vices.

"Overall, my numbers are something like $12 billion would be saved from not enforcing marijuana laws," says Miron, "and $7 billion could be collected in revenue, assuming it's taxed at something like the rates on alcohol and tobacco."

The numbers are "not totally trivial," he concedes. "But when we're looking at a $1.84 trillion deficit, a net of $15 to $20 billion seems like a rounding error."

For that reason, he doesn't foresee legalization for tax revenue alone. "I think that would be a reinforcing effect, but I think there's got to be more of an attitude [shift] that, if people can do something without harming other people, it shouldn't matter what that thing is. I think if people don't feel comfortable with it for some broader perspective, $15 billion isn't going to change their minds."

Prohibition and Violence

If dollar signs don't convince the anti-pot lobby, then how about the fact that Mexican drug cartels are appropriating public land in Western states to grow bushels of marijuana? Or the fact that ever more US officials, from Homeland Security Secretary Janet Napolitano to Joint Chiefs of Staff Chairman Mike Mullen, are fearing spillover of the cartels' grisly violence—more than 6,000 murders last year—into Tuscon and El Paso?

"If drugs were legal, that would not be happening," says Dan Baum, whose 1997 book, *Smoke and Mirrors: The War on Drugs and the Politics of Failure*, is considered one of the best chronicles of the drug war's litany of failures. "It's a misapprehension of the truth to say that the violence in Mexico is because of American appetite for drugs. It's not the appetite for drugs—it's the prohibition that's causing the violence."

Certainly, these cartels traffic in some very bad stuff: heroin, methamphetamine, cocaine. But, says Nadelmann, "half of the Mexican drug gangs' revenue comes from marijuana. Legalizing marijuana is a pretty powerful way of depriving these gangsters of revenue—the same way we took [gangster] Al Capone and those guys out."

Prohibitionists are at a loss for a coherent argument when it comes to the cartels, argues Mirken. "They'll say really dumb things like 'Legalizing marijuana isn't going to make these gangs turn into law-abiding citizens.' No, of course not! It will make them irrelevant! Just like you don't need bootleggers when you have Anheuser-Busch."

More and more credible people are echoing the sentiment. In January, Arizona attorney general Goddard opined that legalization "could certainly cut the legs off of some of these criminal activities." In February, former presidents Ernesto Zedillo Ponce de León of Mexico, Fernando Henrique Cardoso of Brazil, and César Gaviria [Trujillo] of Colombia gathered at the Latin American Commission on Drugs and Democracy and called for decriminalization, decrying the fact that "current policies are based on prejudices and fears and not on results."

Just last week, former Mexican president Vicente Fox put it plainly: "I believe it's time to open the debate over legalizing drugs."

That debate, at least, is happening in earnest. What it leads to is another matter. In the meantime, says Mirken, "We are effectively subsidizing these horrible Mexican gangs by handing them the marijuana market."

People are much more comfortable with the idea of smoking marijuana than they once were.

The Rise in Pro-Legalization Sentiment

Of course, it's not just Mexican presidents who are honest about drugs. American ones can also be pretty, er, blunt. "I inhaled frequently," then candidate Obama admitted last year when asked if he had ever smoked pot. "That was the point."

To see how far we've come, consider the fact that, just 17 years ago, candidate Bill Clinton felt compelled to fudge his answer to that same question with his own infamous equivocation. Or that, 22 years ago, Douglas Ginsburg's admission to smoking pot cost him a Supreme Court seat.

People are much more comfortable with the idea of smoking marijuana than they once were. The media may have brewed up a tempest in a teapot when [Olympian] Michael Phelps was photographed with a bong held to his lips, and cereal giant Kellogg's may have voided his sponsorship deal in a panic. But most Americans couldn't give a fig.

"I do think it's begun to sink in for people now that the last three presidents have smoked marijuana," says Mirken. "As has the governor of California, the mayor of New York City, the guy [Phelps] who's won more Olympic gold medals than anyone on the planet."

Meanwhile, more and more people polled are comfortable expressing pro-legalization sentiments. "We've seen the numbers jump quite dramatically in the past six months to a year," says Nadelmann. "It's really quite something."

In February, Silver looked at the results of three polls (Rasmussen, CBS, Zogby) on Fivethirtyeight.com, each of which found 40 percent or more of respondents supporting legalization. That "may be significant" he allowed, but cautioned against overexuberance. None of this promises upward movement.

"On issues like this, yes, there are trends, but they're not necessarily inevitable," he says now. "If you were looking at the world in the 1960s, you may well have guessed that, by 2009, you'd be able to smoke pot legally."

But that didn't happen. After the '70s came the '80s. A crack epidemic. A crime wave. Nancy Reagan and "Just Say No." Moods can change. And if the pot issue moves unduly forward, wonders Silver, "Will the Republicans try to create a backlash on that and say, 'We've gone too far?' I think it's not totally out of the question, if the economy stays in the dumps for a period of months or years," he adds, "that the crime rate may increase again and that may work against legalization and harm that momentum a bit."

But generational shifts happen. And now, with most people under the age of 65 probably at least familiar with the pungent smoky odor, the trend *should* continue toward increased acceptance. Writing on Fivethirtyeight.com, Silver predicted that "we'll need to see a supermajority of Americans" favoring legalization before politicians would be emboldened enough to press the issue.

He crunched the numbers and figured that, assuming the trend kept heading northward, we could reach 60 percent or so sometime in the next 13 years, predicts Silver. "I feel comfortable with 2022."

The Importance of "Coming Out"

In the past decade and a half, 13 states have legalized medical marijuana, a steady drip that is somewhat analogous—in its suddenness and once-seeming-improbability—to the snowballing momentum of gay marriage rulings over the past several months.

"There's a powerful analogy between the gay rights movement and the marijuana law reform movement," says Nadelmann. "Part of it is about a principle—that people should not be punished for what they do in their own home or their own personal lives. The other point is that there's an element of 'coming out' that is pivotal to the whole process of decriminalizing and ultimately legalizing the behavior."

Atlantic writer Andrew Sullivan has done a fine job of hammering this point again and again over the past couple months on his blog *The Daily Dish*, both with his own thoughtful analysis and in a series of posts tagged "The Cannabis Closet," in which he publishes mostly anonymous responses from his readers. "Contract manager with a government agency [and] Treasurer for the PTA" one describes himself. "If I got busted, I'd lose a lot," writes another.

"I truly believe that if marijuana users felt as emboldened to come out as gay and lesbian people did some years ago," says Nadelmann, "marijuana prohibition would come crashing down very quickly." The problem is that "it's hard to get people to come out of the closet about something that does remain a crime."

There are "millions of Americans who smoke marijuana for whom it's not a problem, who are part of the middle class, who are well-off, who are role models," says Mirken. Most people know this. Yet still the caricature persists of the feckless stoner, slack-jawed and speckled with Pringles crumbs.

As long as the sorts of people who write into Sullivan's blog can't come out and correct that stereotype—as Mirken says, "The only people who end up coming out are the ones who show up at the hemp fests and get in trouble"—the battle for wider acceptance will be a hard slog.

The endgame of pot advocates is to abolish federal prohibition, just as was done with alcohol in 1933.

Slowly, state by state, that may be changing. One Massachusetts reader e-mailed *The Daily Dish* to say that the Bay State's recent decriminalization "has also allowed me to 'come out' publicly as a smoker. When I go out for drinks with coworkers and they comment on my lack of drinks, I simply say that I prefer marijuana because it's less debilitating (at least for me). This still takes people aback a bit, but they'll get used to it."

The End of Federal Prohibition

Whether our representatives in Washington will be brave enough to embrace this emerging political sentiment remains to be seen. "While in general I don't think the criticism that

'Politicians are lagging the public in enlightenment' is accurate," says Frank, "I do think it's true in this case." . . .

Ultimately, whether it's in 2016 or 2022—or even sooner—the endgame of pot advocates is to abolish federal prohibition, just as was done with alcohol in 1933, and to allow states to draft their own laws—whatever they may be.

"That may mean that Mississippi stays dry for another 30 years, as was the case with alcohol," explains Nadelmann. "It may mean that California or Nevada allow marijuana to be sold round the clock in corner stores. And it may mean that some other state allows marijuana to be sold legally, but only in the equivalent of the New Hampshire or Utah state-licensed liquor outlets."

"I think in five years, more states will be doing what Massachusetts is doing," says Frank. "And I'm hoping within 10 that the federal government will get smart and allow the state to do what it wants to do."

Meanwhile, it's hard not to feel like we're heading in the right direction. But it's important to keep pressing the issue. [Board member of MassCann/NORML Mike] Crawford notes that he and his fellow activists have been redoubling their efforts lately. Otherwise, he says, there's no telling when "this window may be gone."

As anyone forced by prohibition to smoke on the sly knows, it's best to keep the window open.

CHAPTER 4

What Are the Effects of State Medical Marijuana Laws?

Overview: State Medical Marijuana Laws

Mark Eddy

Mark Eddy is a specialist in social policy for the Congressional Research Service, the public policy research arm of the US Congress.

In the face of federal intransigence on the issue, advocates of medical marijuana have turned to the states in a largely successful effort, wherever it has been attempted, to enact laws that enable patients to obtain and use botanical marijuana therapeutically in a legal and regulated manner, even though such activity remains illegal under federal law.

States Allowing Use of Medical Marijuana

Fourteen states, covering about 27% of the U.S. population, have enacted laws to allow the use of cannabis for medical purposes. These states have removed state-level criminal penalties for the cultivation, possession, and use of medical marijuana, if such use has been recommended by a medical doctor. All of these states have in place, or are developing, programs to regulate the use of medical marijuana by approved patients. Physicians in these states are immune from liability and prosecution for discussing or recommending medical cannabis to their patients in accordance with state law. Patients in state programs (except for New Mexico and New Jersey) may be assisted by caregivers—persons who are authorized to help patients grow, acquire, and use the drug.

Mark Eddy, "State and Local Referenda and Legislation," *Medical Marijuana: Review and Analysis of Federal and State Policies*, CRS Report for Congress, Congressional Research Service, April 2, 2010, p. 17–22. Courtesy of Congressional Research Service.

Nine of the 14 states that have legalized medical marijuana are in the West: Alaska, California, Colorado, Hawaii, Montana, Nevada, New Mexico, Oregon, and Washington. Of the 37 states outside the West, Michigan plus four other states, all in the Northeast—Maine, New Jersey, Rhode Island, and Vermont—have adopted medical cannabis statutes. Hawaii, New Jersey, New Mexico, Rhode Island, and Vermont have the only programs created by acts of their state legislatures. The medical marijuana programs in the other nine states were approved by the voters in statewide referenda or ballot initiatives, beginning in 1996 with California. Since then, voters have approved medical marijuana initiatives in every state where they have appeared on the ballot with the exception of South Dakota, where a medical marijuana initiative was defeated in 2006 by 52% of the voters. Bills to create medical marijuana programs have been introduced in the legislatures of additional states—Alabama, Arizona, Connecticut, Illinois, Maryland, Minnesota, and New Hampshire, among others—and have received varying levels of consideration but have so far not been enacted.

Effective state medical marijuana laws do not attempt to overturn or otherwise violate federal laws that prohibit doctors from writing prescriptions for marijuana and pharmacies from distributing it. In the 14 states with medical marijuana programs, doctors do not actually prescribe marijuana, and the marijuana products used by patients are not distributed through pharmacies. Rather, doctors *recommend* marijuana to their patients, and the cannabis products are grown by patients or their caregivers, or they are obtained from cooperatives or other alternative dispensaries. The state medical marijuana programs do, however, contravene the federal prohibition of marijuana. Medical marijuana patients, their caregivers, and other marijuana providers can, therefore, be arrested by federal law enforcement agents, and they can be prosecuted under federal law.

Statistics on Medical Marijuana Users

Determining exactly how many patients use medical marijuana with state approval is difficult, but the limited data available suggest the number is rising rapidly. According to a 2002 study published in the *Journal of Cannabis Therapeutics*, an estimated 30,000 California patients and another 5,000 patients in eight other states possessed physicians' recommendations to use cannabis medically. The *New England Journal of Medicine* reported in August 2005 that an estimated 115,000 people had obtained marijuana recommendations from doctors in the states with programs.

Although 115,000 people might have been approved medical marijuana users in 2005, the number of patients who had actually registered was much lower. A July 2005 CRS [Congressional Research Service] telephone survey of the state programs revealed a total of 14,758 registered medical marijuana users in eight states. (Maine and Washington do not maintain state registries, and Rhode Island, New Mexico, Michigan, and New Jersey had not yet passed their laws.) This number vastly understated the actual number of medical marijuana users, however, because California's state registry was in pilot status, with only 70 patients so far registered.

More recently an estimate published by *Newsweek* early in 2010 found a total of 369,634 users in the 13 states with established programs, with California's estimated patient population of 253,800 alone accounting for 69% of the total. (It remains necessary to estimate California's number because registration is voluntary at both the state and county levels, and only a small fraction of patients choose to register. There were fewer than 33,000 registered patients as of March 2010, according to the state's medical marijuana program website.)

A brief description of each state's medical marijuana program follows. The programs are discussed in the order in which they were approved by voters or became law by actions of the state legislatures.

California (1996). Proposition 215 [the Compassionate Use Act of 1996], approved by 56% of the voters in November, removed the state's criminal penalties for medical marijuana use, possession, and cultivation by patients with the "written or oral recommendation or approval of a physician" who has determined that the patient's "health would benefit from medical marijuana." Called the Compassionate Use Act, it legalized cannabis for "the treatment of cancer, anorexia, AIDS, chronic pain, spasticity, glaucoma, arthritis, migraine, or any other illness for which marijuana provides relief." The law permits possession of an amount sufficient for the patient's "personal medical purposes." A second statute (Senate bill 420), passed in 2003, allows "reasonable compensation" for medical marijuana caregivers and states that the drug should be distributed on a nonprofit basis.

Oregon (1998). Voters in November removed the state's criminal penalties for use, possession, and cultivation of marijuana by patients whose physicians advise that marijuana "may mitigate the symptoms or effects" of a debilitating condition. The law, approved by 55% of Oregon voters, does not provide for distribution of cannabis but allows up to seven plants per patient (changed to 24 plants by act of the state legislature in 2005). The state registry program is supported by patient fees. (In the November 2004 election, 58% of Oregon voters rejected a measure that would have expanded the state's existing program.)

Alaska (1998). Voters in November approved a ballot measure to remove state-level criminal penalties for patients diagnosed by a physician as having a debilitating medical condition for which other approved medications were considered. The measure was approved by 58% of the voters. In 1999, the state legislature created a mandatory state registry for medical cannabis users and limited the amount a patient can legally possess to 1 ounce and six plants.

Washington (1998). Approved in November by 59% of the voters, the ballot initiative exempts from prosecution patients who meet all qualifying criteria, possess no more marijuana than is necessary for their own personal medical use (but no more than a 60-day supply), and present valid documentation to investigating law enforcement officers. The state does not issue identification cards to patients.

Maine (1999). Maine's ballot initiative, passed in November by 61% of the voters, puts the burden on the state to prove that a patient's medical use or possession is not authorized by statute. Patients with a qualifying condition, authenticated by a physician, who have been "advised" by the physician that they "might benefit" from medical cannabis, are permitted 1 1/4 ounces and six plants. There is no state registry of patients.

Hawaii (2000). In June, the Hawaii legislature approved a bill removing state-level criminal penalties for medical cannabis use, possession, and cultivation of up to seven plants. A physician must certify that the patient has a debilitating condition for which "the potential benefits of the medical use of marijuana would likely outweigh the health risks." This was the first state law permitting medical cannabis use that was enacted by a legislature instead of by ballot initiative.

Colorado (2000). A ballot initiative to amend the state constitution was approved by 54% of the voters in November. The amendment provides that lawful medical cannabis users must be diagnosed by a physician as having a debilitating condition and be "advised" by the physician that the patient "might benefit" from using the drug. A patient and the patient's caregiver may possess 2 usable ounces and six plants.

Nevada (2000). To amend the state constitution by ballot initiative, a proposed amendment must be approved by the voters in two separate elections. In November, 65% of Nevada voters passed for the second time an amendment to exempt medical cannabis users from prosecution. Patients who have "written documentation" from their physicians that marijuana may alleviate their health condition may register with the state Department of Agriculture and receive an identification card that exempts them from state prosecution for using medical marijuana.

Vermont (2004). In May, Vermont became the second state to legalize medical cannabis by legislative action instead of ballot initiative. Vermont patients are allowed to grow up to three marijuana plants in a locked room and to possess 2 ounces of manicured marijuana under the supervision of the Department of Public Safety, which maintains a patient registry. The law went into effect without the signature of the governor, who declined to sign it but also refused to veto it, despite pressure from Washington. A 2007 legislative act expanded eligibility for the program and increased to nine the number of plants participants may grow.

Montana (2004). In November, 62% of state voters passed Initiative 148 [the Montana Medical Marijuana Act], allowing qualifying patients to use marijuana under medical supervision. Eligible medical conditions include cancer, glaucoma, HIV/AIDS, wasting syndrome, seizures, and severe or chronic pain. A doctor must certify that the patient has a debilitating medical condition and that the benefits of using marijuana would likely outweigh the risks. The patient may grow up to six plants and possess 1 ounce of dried marijuana. The state public health department registers patients and caregivers.

Rhode Island (2006). In January, the state legislature overrode the governor's veto of a medical marijuana bill, allowing patients to possess up to 12 plants or 2 1/2 ounces to treat cancer, HIV/AIDS, and other chronic ailments. The law included a sunset provision and was set to expire on July 1, 2007, unless renewed by the legislature. The law was made permanent on June 21, 2007, after legislators voted again to override the governor's veto by a wide margin.

New Mexico (2007). Passed by the legislature and signed into law by the governor in April, the Lynn and Erin Compassionate Use Act went into effect on July 1, 2007. It requires the state's Department of Health to set rules governing the distribution of medical cannabis to state-authorized patients. Unlike most other state programs, patients and their caregivers cannot grow their own marijuana; rather, it will be provided by state-licensed "cannabis production facilities."

Michigan (2008). Approved by 63% of Michigan voters in the November 2008 presidential election, Proposal 1 permits physicians to approve marijuana use by registered patients with debilitating medical conditions, including cancer, HIV/AIDS, hepatitis C, multiple sclerosis, glaucoma, and other conditions approved by the state's Department of Community Health. Up to 12 plants can be cultivated in an indoor, locked facility by the patient or a designated caregiver.

New Jersey (2010). A bill passed by the legislature and signed by the governor allows for the regulated distribution of marijuana by state-monitored dispensaries. Doctors may recommend up to 2 ounces monthly to registered patients, who are not allowed to grow their own. Considered the most restrictive of the state programs approved to date, the law restricts usage to a specific set of diseases including cancer, AIDS, glaucoma, muscular dystrophy, multiple sclerosis, and other diseases involving severe and chronic pain, severe nausea, seizures, or severe and persistent muscle spasms.

State Legalization of Medical Marijuana Has Led to Misguided Local Regulation

Travis Kavulla

Travis Kavulla is a writer and former associate editor of the National Review.

They could barely have looked worse. An out-of-towner from Missoula, the "progressive" enclave of Montana, sang the praises of his large-scale marijuana grow operation. A "patient" swayed side to side as she discussed her long acquaintance with heroin and meth—that is, before she mellowed out with the help of pot. In the back, some pale and hollow-looking youths lurked, and the mayor, catching their eyes, insisted that they remove their hats. They stared sullenly back at him for a while, mumbled, and complied. A dwarf who makes a living as a cannabis cultivator rose to deride the commission meeting. "This is a circus!" he bellowed. This rabble needed a lobbyist.

Medical Marijuana in Montana

The potheads had shown up in droves at hearings of the Great Falls City Commission, which this month [March 2010] imposed a moratorium on "caregivers"—as legal dealers are known in the patois of Montana's medical marijuana law. The moratorium notionally prevents anyone from making a profit off the legal marijuana trade. The city says the ban is intended to be temporary, awaiting the formulation of permanent zoning regulations.

"Medical marijuana" has been legal in Montana since 2004. As in Colorado, California, and Oregon, the vehicle was a

Travis Kavulla, "Zoned Out: In Montana, Medical Marijuana Regulation Threatens to Shut Down the Most Legitimate Tier of Operators," *National Review*, vol. 62, no. 5, March 22, 2010, p. 24. Reproduced by permission.

voter initiative—marijuana activists gathered signatures to qualify it for the ballot and then made a campaign pitch that had something to do with dying grandmas and cancer. In Montana, the Medical Marijuana Act passed with 62 percent of the vote, outpacing even George W. Bush, who took the Treasure State's electoral votes with 59 percent.

The law provides for virtually no regulation. A single state employee is tasked with the administration and enforcement of the program, even though a robust industry has grown around the law, with doctors to prescribe and legal pot dealers to provide. Traveling clinics fan out from Missoula to other Montana towns, doctors and "caregivers" in tow. At a local hotel on a crisp fall day last year, my friends and I were about to get a drink. Walking in, we passed a sign with a marijuana leaf and, our interest piqued, went into a conference room where jars of marijuana buds sat on a table. One expects this type of thing in Oakland, but here in Montana? It still takes a moment to get beyond the unreality of it all.

De Facto Legalization

Jason Christ, owner of the Montana Caregivers Network, stood in the hotel lobby, shod in Birkenstocks. More than anyone, he is the face of medical marijuana in Montana—photographed by the local newspaper puffing away on a joint on the steps of the Civic Center, or testifying to anyone with ears to hear (public bodies and journalists mostly) about his case of celiac disease and the resulting hemorrhoids which, he says, drove him to marijuana use.

He gave our group of four the once-over and perhaps we twentysomethings looked unduly sickly, because he urged all of us to sign up. My friend, who suffers from knee pain and an allergy to government regulation, paid the $150 "consulting fee" on a lark. Not more than ten minutes later, and with no examination of his medical file, a physician had signed his medical marijuana form. This year, the Caregivers Network began to offer doctor evaluations via webcam, and it contracts with a team of six lawyers to head off trouble. When my friend received his "green card" from the state of Montana, its text was slanted due to printer error. But no matter. Here was a ticket to ride.

The word is out about "medical" marijuana, passed along the street and, increasingly, by mass media.

For those potheads clever enough to go through this mild process of state-sanctioned fibbing, the medical marijuana law has meant the de facto legalization of the drug. Paul Gorsuch, a neurosurgeon at Benefis [Health System] in Great Falls, says he has seen many of his patients obtain green cards. About 25 percent of medical marijuana patients are between 21 and 30, according to the state's Department of Public Health and Human Services. Dr. Gorsuch says that "the age breakdown fits a recreational-use model," not one aligned to the incidence of the diseases and chronic pain marijuana is used to manage. He suspects that some in his profession are abetting fraud.

After four years of quiet use and abuse through this rubric, last year ushered in a bonanza of legal marijuana use. Of the state's more than 8,000 registered patients, 2,800 were issued green cards in the last two months of 2009. By the end of the year, the number of cardholders had increased sixfold.

A Growing Industry

The word is out about "medical" marijuana, passed along the street and, increasingly, by mass media. Suggestive ads for caregivers appear every week in newspapers across the state. The subdued caregiver table at the one-day clinic, with its pre-scheduled medical interviews, has been supplanted by an almost carnival-esque atmosphere, twinkling with canning jars full of marijuana and fanciful smoking implements, where a wink and a nod suffice to inveigle a doctor's approval. These events, which once drew dozens, today attract hundreds.

Here in the state's third-largest city, 24-year-old Brandon Peressini saw in medical marijuana an industry full of opportunity. Last June, he took out space in a former Catholic hospital, now an office building. Since, he has gardened marijuana in two basement rooms, selling to nearly 150 patients. He says he knows all their names and conditions. On an upper floor of the building, Peressini keeps a demure, sparsely furnished counseling office—"as personable a place," he says, "as any dentist office or community clinic." It is hard to disagree. During the course of my recent visit to the facility in the company of a city commissioner—Peressini welcomes all comers—a neighboring tenant cheerfully popped in to say hello.

"In the six months we've been in operation, we never heard one word of complaint from other tenants," Peressini says. His landlord, moreover, has no problem with the operation and even agreed to finance a $150,000 renovation of the stately but mouldering building's seventh floor to accommodate an expansion of Peressini's business. . . . Peressini says he'll require about 3,000 square feet, and he has even recruited an architect whose credits include Montana State's plant-research facility to conduct the redesign of this old nunnery, which has been vacant for two decades.

A Local Attempt to Regulate

Trouble began for Peressini when he sent in his application for a fire-safety inspection certificate, an act many businesses in his building did not even bother complying with. Nonetheless, it is the law, and Peressini attempted to follow it. The municipal ordinance book said nothing about marijuana zoning—and in zoning theory, when the law says nothing, all is allowed. But a month after Peressini applied, the city returned his application and filing fee. Attached was a sticky note from a community planning director, informing him to shut down his operation.

The next Peressini heard of it, the city attorney was bemoaning the dangers of mold and carbon dioxide gassing supposedly associated with cannabis cultivation and speculating on the threat of blight that dispensaries pose to the community. Medical marijuana may have been passed as a state law by the voters, but throughout the West cities are adopting strict zoning laws that shut down the legal marijuana business.

Whether they are frauds or not, revoking their smoking rights is not within a local government's purview.

"Bulls**t," says Mary Jolley, the city commissioner who visited Peressini's with me, when I ask her about the "blight" argument during a winter meeting of the Montana Republican Party. She contends that the problems concerning marijuana are being blown out of proportion merely to give the city a pretext to regulate. "I oppose creating special categories for persons who are using a legal product, legally purchased and sold and grown," says Jolley, who leans libertarian and was on the losing end of the 4-1 vote to retroactively ban all medical marijuana businesses, including those that had already applied for city permits.

Unwarranted Regulation

Peressini . . . has put his renovation plans on hold for the moment, but he still talks dreamily of buying a device that measures THC [tetrahydrocannabinol] content in marijuana so that it can be further formalized, quantified, as a legitimate drug. Other large marijuana businesses in the state meticulously inventory and invoice their product. Caregivers frequently call for their produce to be taxed. For now, Peressini merrily operates in defiance of the city ban, and as he waits for zoning regulations to be finalized, he says he is contemplating taking his outfit across the county line or simply to an undisclosed location.

In many western states today, a considerable number of people have a legal right to grow, sell, possess, and consume marijuana. Whether they are frauds or not, revoking their smoking rights is not within a local government's purview, and state legislatures have been reluctant to rescind what the voters have passed through the initiative process. One way or another, these legal users will conduct their trade. Either the legal marijuana business will be carried out in the light of day, in a storefront business or other commercial property; or, if such properties are zoned out, users will revert to the template of the furtive drug deal. Here in Montana, regulation has tended to clamp a vise around the most legitimate tier of operators.

Legal Medical Marijuana Has Caused Problems for Local Communities

Bill Croke

Bill Croke is a writer who frequently contributes to the American Spectator.

According to the Great Falls, Montana, *Tribune*, at an October 2009 medical marijuana health screening in that city, a Dr. Patricia Cole of Whitefish examined 150 patients in 14 and a half hours. That's an average of one every six minutes. Dr. Cole is affiliated with the Missoula-based "Montana Caregivers Network" (MCN), which promotes the traveling "Cannabis Caravans" in the Treasure State. And these aren't conducted in hospitals or clinic settings. They can be set up in a conference room in a local hotel. For a fee ($150, or $100 for veterans and low-income people) a doctor examines you and decides if you are eligible—depending on your specific physical or psychological complaint—for a card that permits you to be prescribed medical marijuana from a personal "caregiver." Some submitted paperwork and payment for the "examination" and an additional $25 registration fee is all it takes to be issued a card, as no formal medical records are required, only a stated complaint such as chronic headaches or insomnia or back pain. And a card permits not only access to the marijuana retail outlets and licensed caregivers, but also allows one to grow a limited amount of the weed for one's own use.

The Legalization of Medical Marijuana in Montana

The *Tribune* goes on to relate that the Montana Board of Medical Examiners has frowned on Dr. Cole's entrepreneurial

Bill Croke, "High Under the Big Sky," *American Spectator*, June 2, 2010. www.spectator
.org. Reproduced by permission.

adventures amongst the stoners, and fined her $2,000 for promoting "inadequate standards of care." It further noted that Dr. Cole "did not document medical histories [or] discuss proper dosing . . . [or] document a risk analysis of medical marijuana." Dr. Cole is Montana's first physician to be so disciplined. The Montana Caregivers Network supplied her with legal counsel and paid her fine. The above is illustrative of the problems Montana is now dealing with as a poorly written law light on regulation is currently implemented.

Small municipalities lack the law enforcement capability to deal with criminality related to the dispensing of medical marijuana.

In 2004, 62% of Treasure State voters approved Initiative 148 [the Montana Medical Marijuana Act], which legalized medical marijuana for "certified patients" with a "debilitating medical condition" (i.e., cancer, AIDS, glaucoma, etc.). In October 2009, the [Barack] Obama administration ordered federal prosecutors to cease prosecuting medical marijuana patients in the legalized states. Montana—one of fourteen states and the District of Columbia to have legalized medical marijuana—now has 15,000 registered "patients," up from 3,000 a year ago [June 2009]. It turns out there [are] a lot of sick folks riding the Cannabis Caravan in Montana. "Before the doors even open the parking lot has 300 kids throwing Frisbees and playing Hacky Sack," Mark Long, narcotics chief for the Montana Department of Justice told the *Wall Street Journal [WSJ]*.

The Problems Caused by Legal Marijuana

However, the brave new world of medicinal dope has a darker side than hippies tossing around Frisbees. In Kalispell a man was murdered who was tied to the theft of medical marijuana. There have been related assaults in the Missoula area. In Billings, Montana's largest city, there have been two firebombings of medical marijuana outlets and "Not in our town" spray painted on the walls. The Billings City Council, with 80 licensed weed dispensaries already in the city of 100,000, has lately instituted a six-month moratorium on an additional 25 more. "It's an absolute nightmare," Billings Mayor Tom Hanel told the *WSJ*. "My prediction is that it's only going to get worse if we continue to allow it." Kalispell and Great Falls have also followed the moratorium route, as have the small towns of Anaconda near Butte, and Cascade near Great Falls. These last two (and scores of others in the state) underscore the simple fact that small municipalities lack the law enforcement capability to deal with criminality related to the dispensing of medical marijuana. And here's an interesting set of statistics: Montana has roughly 1,000 licensed pharmacies, from small town drugstores to those found in chain retail stores such as Walmart; and in the last few years it's accumulated 5,000 caregivers (mostly growing marijuana at home) and storefront outlets. And another: 9% of Montanans on probation or on parole from the state correctional system are in possession of medical marijuana cards.

Los Angeles has now started to tightly regulate medical weed, and is closing many outlets ... that are home to criminal activity and gang infiltration.

The Montana Caregivers Network is an interesting entity. It's a nonprofit whose executive director Jason Christ is the poster boy for medical marijuana in the Treasure State. Christ has attracted much media attention leading "smoke-ins" around the state, where he has made a show of lighting up in front of the State Capitol in Helena and within sight of police headquarters in Missoula. For Christ, medical marijuana (and it would seem legalization in general) is a public crusade. A typical quote: "I honestly feel like this has become a civil rights issue." MCN has recently instituted online "TeleClinics," physician exams via webcam; that is, it is now possible to access the Cannabis Caravan via cyberspace. That'll certainly save MCN rental fees for all those hotel conference rooms. But one wonders what the Montana Board of Medical Examiners thinks of such an impersonal and medically unethical doctor-patient encounter?

The Dichotomy of Urban and Small Towns

There is a definite dichotomy seen in Montana's medical marijuana controversy. Initiative 148 was very popular in urban Montana; cities such as Billings, Helena, Great Falls, Butte, and the liberal college towns of Missoula and Bozeman. Not so much in small towns across the vast rural reaches of the Treasure State. Urban Montana mustered the votes to pass 148. What is it about medical weed and university towns, not only in Montana, but across the country?

Missoula, population 70,000, is home to the University of Montana. There are a dozen storefront outlets and 400 registered caregiver/growers serving 1,800 (and growing) card carriers. According to a story in the *Missoulian*, many residents laud the fact that medical marijuana is giving a previously moribund commercial real estate market a boost, as more storefront outlets open. And garden supply stores are booming. Bozeman, population 35,000, and home to Montana State University, has 500 caregivers. One in 70 people in Bozeman is a caregiver. These are two cities populated for much of the year by thousands of young, vigorously healthy college students. Maybe there's a high rate of card carriers among the more long-in-the-tooth administrations and faculties.

The Future of Montana's Law

Montana seems to be learning the lessons of California, a state always incubating bad ideas. After a decade of dispensary expansion, Los Angeles has now started to tightly regulate medical weed, and is closing many outlets (L.A. has more of these than it has Starbucks) that are home to criminal activity and gang infiltration. Missoula isn't Los Angeles, but the same sort of problems are already cropping up there.

The Montana state legislature will join the fray during its next session in January 2011, when it will take up legislative reform related to filling the many abuse-ridden regulatory holes in the 2004 initiative. And there are calls from some of its Republican members to simply repeal the whole mess. So the question remains: Who—if anybody—will be permitted to get high under the Big Sky?

The Fight Against Medical Marijuana Will Determine the Fate of Legalization

Brian Doherty

Brian Doherty is a senior editor at Reason *magazine and Reason.com.*

Newsweek dubbed Los Angeles "the wild West of weed" in October 2009, and that phrase often echoed through the city council's chamber as it haggled over a long-awaited ordinance regulating the dispensaries. Both the *Los Angeles Times* and the *LA Weekly* regularly jabbed at the city council for fiddling while marijuana burned, supplied by storefront pot dispensaries that were widely (but inaccurately) said to total 1,000 or more.

The Reasoning Behind Regulation

On January 26 [2010], after years of dithering and months of debate, the city council finally passed an ordinance to regulate medical marijuana shops. In addition to dictating the details of lighting, record keeping, auditing, bank drops, hours of operation, and compensation for owners and employees, the ordinance requires a dramatic reduction in the number of dispensaries. The official limit is 70, but because of exemptions for some preexisting dispensaries the final number could grow as high as 137. The ordinance allocates the surviving dispensaries among the city's "planning districts" and requires that they be located more than 1,000 feet from each other and from "sensitive areas" such as parks, schools, churches, and libraries. It also requires patients who obtain marijuana from dispensaries to pick one outlet and stick with it.

As those rules suggest, city officials are not prepared to treat marijuana like any other medicine, despite a 1996 state

Brian Doherty, "L.A.'s Pot Revolution," *Reason*, May 2010. Reproduced by permission.

ballot initiative that allows patients with doctors' recommendations to use it for symptom relief. It's hard to imagine the city council arbitrarily limiting the number of pharmacies, insisting that they not do business near competitors, creating buffer zones between parks and Duane Read [a pharmacy chain] locations, or demanding that patients obtain their Lipitor from one and only one drugstore. Such restrictions reflect marijuana's dual identity in California: It is simultaneously medicine and menace. At the same time, the regulations do serve to legitimize distribution of a drug that remains completely prohibited by federal law—a stamp of approval welcomed by many dispensary operators.

When I asked activists, businessmen, or politicians why L.A.'s medical marijuana market needed to be regulated, they almost invariably replied, "It was unregulated." When I delved beyond that tautology, I found motives little different from those that drive land use planning generally. The activists who demanded that the city bring order to the "wild West" of medical marijuana were motivated not by antipathy to cannabis so much as mundane concerns about "blight," neighborhood character, and spillover effects. While responding to these concerns, every member of the city council voiced support for medical access to marijuana in theory, and none openly sided with the federal law enforcement officials who view the trade as nothing more than drug dealing in disguise.

The strife in pot-saturated Los Angeles has had more to do with land use regulation than with eradicating an allegedly evil plant.

The Resistance to Marijuana Normalization

Los Angeles became the medical marijuana capital of America thanks to a combination of entrepreneurial energy and benign political neglect. What happened here is instructive for other jurisdictions that already or may soon let patients use the drug. In the last 14 years, the voters or legislators of 14 states and the District of Columbia have legalized marijuana for at least some medical purposes. Medical marijuana campaigns, via either legislation or ballot initiative, are active in 13 other states. National surveys indicate broad public support for such reforms. An ABC News/*Washington Post* poll conducted in January [2010] found that 81 percent of Americans think patients who can benefit from marijuana should be able to obtain it legally.

But L.A.'s experience also shows that majority support for medical marijuana is not necessarily enough. An October [2009] poll of Los Angeles residents commissioned by the Marijuana Policy Project found that 77 percent supported regulating dispensaries, while only 14 percent wanted them closed. But patients and the entrepreneurs who served them still had to contend with a noisy minority, clustered in political institutions such as neighborhood councils, the police department, and government lawyers' offices, who resisted the normalization of marijuana. That process culminated in an ordinance with onerous restrictions that could nearly eliminate the current medical pot business and cause great hardship for tens of thousands of Los Angeles residents who use marijuana as a medicine.

Still, for those who lived through the ferocious cultural and political war over pot during the second half of the 20th century, it's amazing that the strife in pot-saturated Los Angeles has had more to do with land use regulation than with eradicating an allegedly evil plant. Even with pot readily available over the counter at hundreds of locations to anyone with an easily obtained doctor's letter, the most common complaints were essentially aesthetic.

The Compassionate Use Act in California

When California voters agreed in 1996 to legalize pot for medical use, the initiative campaign emphasized marijuana's utility in treating AIDS wasting syndrome, the side effects of cancer chemotherapy, and other grave conditions. But the initiative [Proposition 215], known as the Compassionate Use Act, also allowed pot to be recommended for treatment of "any other illness for which marijuana provides relief." That language strongly influenced how the politics and culture of medical marijuana evolved in Los Angeles.

Critics viewed the dispensaries as thinly disguised pot shops that sold marijuana to the general public for recreational as well as medical purposes.

The federal government did not yield to the judgment of California's voters. The [Bill] Clinton administration threatened to prosecute or revoke the prescription privileges of doctors who recommended marijuana, only to be rebuked by a federal appeals court on First Amendment grounds. From the late 1990s into the first year of the [Barack] Obama administration, the Drug Enforcement Administration (DEA) raided medical marijuana growers and suppliers, without regard to whether they were following California law. Last November, the Justice Department instructed U.S. attorneys that they "should not focus federal resources" on "individuals whose actions are in clear and unambiguous compliance with existing state laws providing for the medical use of marijuana." Yet as of February, the DEA was still raiding medical marijuana shops in the L.A. area.

Ambiguity is built into the Justice Department's new policy, thanks to uncertainty over what exactly it means to comply with state law. The Compassionate Use Act allowed patients or their "primary caregivers" to grow marijuana for medical use. The Medical Marijuana Program Act, a law passed by the state legislature that took effect in 2004, imposed limits on how much marijuana patients or their caregivers could possess, while allowing local jurisdictions to establish higher ceilings. In January the California Supreme Court rejected those limits, saying patients should be allowed to have whatever amount is "reasonable" for their medical needs.

The Regulation of Dispensaries

Most important in understanding what happened in Los Angeles, the 2004 law said patients may join together to "collectively or cooperatively" grow marijuana and distribute it to each other. The law did not define collectives or cooperatives, but guidelines issued by Attorney General Jerry Brown in 2008 said they should be deemed legitimate as long as they were operated by patients, served only members of the collective, and did not take in more revenue than was necessary to cover their operating expenses. Ostensibly, the storefront dispensaries that opened in cities such as Los Angeles, San Diego, San Francisco, and Oakland were collectives operated by and for patients, providing them with their medicine as permitted by state law. But given the ease of obtaining a doctor's recommendation and becoming a collective member, critics viewed the dispensaries as thinly disguised pot shops that sold marijuana to the general public for recreational as well as medical purposes.

As you are frequently reminded by people in Los Angeles who are angry about the way the dispensary system developed, Californians who voted for the Compassionate Use Act had in mind patients with cancer, AIDS, or other serious conditions, people who needed marijuana to relieve agonizing pain, fight debilitating nausea, or restore their appetites so they could take in enough nutrition to stay alive. Voters who supported the initiative did not have in mind milder, vaguer, and less verifiable complaints of the sort that seem to be far more common among people with doctor's recommendations. Austin Elguindy, a partner in an L.A. medical pot recommendation practice called Consulting and Care for Wellness, tells me his top three reasons for recommending marijuana are lower back pain, insomnia, and anxiety.

Regulation of the dispensaries was left to local jurisdictions. Some, such as the politically liberal cities of San Francisco, Oakland, and West Hollywood, experienced an early proliferation that was quickly curbed. San Francisco set a limit of 23 dispensaries, while Oakland and West Hollywood each settled on four. About 120 cities banned pot storefronts entirely (although a lawsuit that is before a state appeals court challenges their authority to do so). Los Angeles, by contrast, declined to address pot dispensaries at all. Medical marijuana entrepreneurs began moving into L.A. in 2003. In May 2005, when City Councilman Dennis Zine (a former cop) first asked the police to look into the dispensaries and asked the city attorney's office to help the council draft regulations for them, just a handful were around. By the end of 2006 there were nearly 100.

The Complaints About Dispensaries

Zine blames the delayed reaction on resistance from then City Attorney Rocky Delgadillo. Don Duncan, a leading medical marijuana activist and operator of a West Hollywood dispensary that opened in 2004, also blames the city attorney's office. He says Delgadillo and his successor, Carmen Trutanich, did not want to legitimize an industry they viewed as illegal. Both took the position, contrary to Attorney General Brown's guidelines, that state law does not allow the exchange of medical marijuana for money, no matter how the distributor is organized or labeled. In a January ruling on a civil nuisance case brought by the city attorney's office against a dispensary called Hemp Factory V, a superior court judge agreed with this narrow reading of the law. Joe Elford, a lawyer for the medical marijuana activist group Americans for Safe Access, says this contradicts state appellate decisions that acknowledge the legality of not-for-profit sales.

The complaints that prompted Zine to consider regulating the dispensaries were not terribly alarming. Citizens were annoyed by pot smokers congregating outside dispensaries. Some parents didn't like the message they believed the dispensaries communicated to their kids: that marijuana was an ordinary commodity that could be sold openly without fear of legal repercussions. They also worried that kids might obtain marijuana from patients, which local journalists have found happens occasionally. Mostly, marijuana just kind of freaks some people out.

The Interim Control Ordinance

In August 2007, the city council rushed through an "interim control ordinance" (ICO) that declared a moratorium on new pot shops. The ordinance also required existing dispensaries to submit paperwork proving they had seller's permits from the state Board of Equalization (which expected them to collect taxes on marijuana sales), a tax registration certificate from the city, and a legitimate commercial lease or property deed. One hundred eighty-three dispensaries filed their paperwork before the November 2007 deadline, of which 137 were still operating when the council passed its new regulations in 2010.

By the time the ICO was passed, many dispensaries had been forced to close by the DEA's tactic of sending threatening letters to landlords who rented space to pot shops. Worried that their property would be seized by the federal government, dozens of landlords evicted marijuana dispensaries. Many of these sellers sought to reopen by applying for a "hardship exemption" under the interim control ordinance. The city let the applications pile up without examining them, and dispensary operators who were not in business prior to the moratorium filed the same forms, hoping they could slip by. Many others, known as "rogues" in the medical marijuana community, opened without bothering to file any paperwork.

By mid-2009 hundreds of what came to be known as "post-ICO" pot shops had opened. Local and national media outlets began to notice. In July, a *Wall Street Journal* story looked askance at the "unchecked growth" of pot shops in L.A. In October, the same month *Newsweek* dubbed L.A. "the wild West of weed," a *New York Times* story tut-tutted that there were "more marijuana stores here than public schools." The city council could no longer avoid the issue.

[The Los Angeles ordinance] imposed draconian restrictions with little thought to how they might affect patients who had come to rely on marijuana to relieve their symptoms.

The Los Angeles Ordinance

According to dispensary critic Michael Larsen, Los Angeles was "a national laughingstock" because of the proliferating pot shops. Based on a combination of hysterical hearsay and applications for exemptions that never turned into functioning storefronts, politicians, journalists, and perturbed neighbors were regularly claiming the city had something like 1,000 dispensaries—more than the number of Starbucks locations.

The *LA Weekly*—an alternative paper that might have been expected to side with the dispensaries, especially given how many of their ads fill the paper—helped lead the negative coverage, as part of a general crusade against what it sees as the city government's fecklessness. The paper in November tried to get an accurate count of the dispensaries and found that 540 or so were operating when the council began reconsidering the issue. To a politician who didn't have to worry about where he could obtain a medicine that helped make his life livable, that must have seemed like an awful lot.

Even though the city council had been considering the issue, on and off, for nearly five years, the ordinance it produced after a contentious back and forth between the council and the city attorney's office seemed half-baked in many respects. It imposed draconian restrictions with little thought to how they might affect patients who had come to rely on marijuana to relieve their symptoms.

The Provisions of the Ordinance

Some of the provisions are mild and largely supported by the medical pot community, which was begging for bearable regulations that would legitimize the dispensaries. The relatively uncontroversial requirements include demands for twice-daily bank runs, no plants visible from the street, and unarmed security guards patrolling a two-block radius around each dispensary.

Other provisions seem difficult to enforce and/or comply with, such as the rule that each patient can be a member of no more than one collective (meaning he can obtain marijuana from just one location), a demand that all the pot distributed go through "an independent and certified laboratory" to be checked for pesticides (dispensary operators insist that no such lab exists in Los Angeles), and a requirement that dispensaries store what could amount to tens of thousands of pieces of paper with patient and transaction information in fireproof vaults on site. Most ominously for the future of the medical marijuana business in L.A., the ordinance creates 1,000-foot "buffers" between the dispensaries and a list of "sensitive uses": schools, churches, libraries, parks, youth centers, substance abuse centers, and other pot dispensaries. A last-minute addition to the bill also bans dispensaries from land "abutting" residential property and specifies that "no collective shall be located on a lot ... across the street or alley from ... a residentially zoned lot or a lot improved with residential use."

If the ordinance survives legal challenges and goes into effect, that last provision will force nearly all of the existing dispensaries to move, and they will have few places to go. Almost all of L.A.'s standard commercial space is separated from homes or apartments merely by an alley behind them. In the weeks after the ordinance passed, various sources in the medical marijuana community told me landlords lucky enough to have space that complies with the new rules have tripled their rents and started demanding five-figure "signing fees" from dispensaries scrambling to find new locations. . . .

The malleability of the medical category is a problem.

The Broadness of the Law

California's medical marijuana law created a special category of people who are allowed to do something that others would be arrested for doing, and it gave a guild of licensed professionals the nearly unlimited power to define this category. Although physicians who issue recommendations for nonmedical reasons theoretically can be disciplined by the state medical board, that has happened only 12 times since 1996, and only one doctor lost his license as a result. The discretion permitted by the law is so broad that proving misconduct is very difficult.

That broad discretion helps patients who might be denied their medicine under a stricter regime, and at the same time it helps people who want pot for recreational purposes. Medical marijuana activists often say that *all* marijuana use is essentially medical, if that category is understood to include quotidian psychological and emotional problems that the drug alleviates. If physicians can prescribe pharmaceuticals to treat stress, anxiety, shyness, and depression, the activists say, why can't they recommend marijuana for the same reasons? Stephen Gutwillig, California state director of the Drug Policy Alliance, offers a partly tongue-in-cheek take on the question: Given how bad for your health it is to get caught up in the criminal justice system because you have marijuana, he says, removing that threat is a form of preventive medicine.

Politically, though, the malleability of the medical category is a problem. Anyone who locates a sympathetic, trusting, or simply greedy doctor can obtain the legal right to possess pot in California. That fact, plus the hundreds of outlets that sprang up in Los Angeles to supply those patients, fostered a fairly accurate public perception that during the last few years anyone willing to put in a little effort could travel a short distance and buy pot over the counter.

The Medical Model of Marijuana

The medical model attaches great importance to motive and state of mind, which is why dispensary operators often say, when justifying themselves to politicians or the press, that they're in the business "for the right reasons," unlike some of their competitors. Combined with the federal ban on marijuana, medicalization leads to a world where customers can shop at only one store; where the cash they pay for a product is not the price but a "contribution to the collective"; where businesses are expected to avoid turning a profit; where a medicine is subject to sales tax, unlike other pharmaceuticals, and isn't regulated like any other pharmaceutical; where you are complying with the law if what you possess is "reasonable" related to some need that may have been invented by a doctor to begin with; where it's legal for you to have pot but you are still apt to be arrested for growing or transporting it.

The medical model also fosters a weirdly contradictory attitude toward pot use, one that seemed to animate the *LA Weekly*'s surprisingly negative coverage of the issue: Even people who don't care about pot smoking in general get upset when they think stoners are gaming a system that is supposed to serve patients with doctor-certified needs. The *LA Weekly* angrily reported in November that 70 percent of the people its reporters saw entering dispensaries were "young men—corroborating D.A. [Steve] Cooley's claim that the real market for all this activity is everyday users, not people suffering serious disease." (Medical activists tend to respond to that sort of talk with the riposte that all sorts of maladies for which pot provides relief aren't diagnosable by strangers watching from yards away.) . . .

The Impact on Full Legalization

Is America ready for a world in which pot is as culturally and physically prevalent as it has become in L.A.? In a national Zogby poll conducted in April 2009, 52 percent of respondents supported treating marijuana more or less like alcohol, while other recent polls put the percentage in the 40s. Support for legalization is higher in California: A Field poll of California voters taken the same month as the Zogby survey put support for legalization at 56 percent statewide and 60 percent in Los Angeles County. This fall [2010] we will see whether those opinions translate into voter support for a California ballot initiative that would, at long last, legalize and tax adult possession of marijuana.

Don Duncan, as dean of L.A.'s medical marijuana suppliers and activists, doesn't want to opine about full legalization. But his take on why all sides have fought so ferociously over the city's medical pot ordinance applies to the legalization debate as well. "The normalization of medical marijuana—certain elements in law enforcement and other civic leaders see it as a threat," he says. "If L.A. is in fact a medical marijuana town with safe access regulated, then that ends the debate for California. . . . Once the state's largest and most populated community has sensible regulations, foes of medical cannabis in law enforcement know they've lost the battle in California. They see it as a line in the sand, so ideologically they can't give up L.A. By the same token, that's why ideologically we can't either."

The fight to define what happened in L.A. during the "wild West" days of what amounted to legal over-the-counter pot is the same sort of battle. If the complaints that led to the regulatory crackdown are understood as arising from anti-pot prejudice, NIMBYism [Not In My Back Yard] and the occasional sighting of "undesirables," rather than real threats to public order and safety, it will seem pretty silly to continue spending billions of dollars and millions of man-hours each year to stop people from exchanging money for pot. The accidental result of a city attorney who didn't want to legitimize marijuana and a city council that didn't want to think about it could be the realization that it's better to allow a pot free-for-all than to continue to wage war on marijuana.

Failing to Enforce Federal Marijuana Law Supports Mexican Criminals

John Walters

John Walters is executive vice president of the Hudson Institute and former director of the Office of National Drug Control Policy under President George W. Bush.

In recent months, more Americans have learned what those living on the border have known for several years: The Mexican government is in a deadly fight with extremely violent gangs.

Thousands and thousands of Mexicans were killed last year [2008] and the carnage continues at a shocking rate. Mexican President Felipe Calderón has been deploying security forces, mobilizing billions of dollars in new spending, and launching historic reform and anticorruption initiatives to stop the terrorist-mafias. He has also sought, unprecedented cooperation from us to defeat this common threat.

A Security Crisis in Mexico

The director of national intelligence, Adm. Dennis Blair, recently suggested that the governability of parts of Mexico is in question. It is now beyond question that the threat is a top national security matter for the United States. Calderón's success or failure will profoundly determine the future security of both our countries.

What is the [Barack] Obama administration doing?

The president could have gone to the border to meet President Calderón and visibly demonstrate that we will stand with

John Walters, "Up in Smoke: The Obama Administration Is Scaling Back Support for Mexico's Drug War," *Weekly Standard*, March 16, 2009. www.weeklystandard.com. Reproduced by permission.

him and that the gangs will not prevail. The senior cabinet officers of both countries—State, Defense, Justice, and others—could have met jointly as was done last December [2008] in Washington, renewing a common plan of attack under the new administration to be driven forward at the highest levels. Is the president confused about whether the danger warrants such action? So far, Secretary of Homeland Security Janet Napolitano is clearly working hard on this issue, but the absence of the president and the rest of the cabinet makes her task more difficult.

The administration should be fighting for full funding of the Mérida program of assistance from the United States. Our vital equipment and training will protect innocent lives in both our countries. But the White House has been unengaged as Congress is on a path to cut $100 million in support beyond the $100 million reduction of the last Congress. At a time when Mexico knows as well as we do that Congress is recklessly stimulating and earmarking billions, slashing funding for our national security is grossly irresponsible.

Much of the marijuana sold in the "dispensaries" of California funds the mafias of Mexico.

Congress further proposes to shift to Central America some of the resources needed in Mexico. When is the White House going to point out that resources for Central America will never be adequate if the fight in Mexico fails? Mexico is the center of gravity.

Equally troubling, the Obama administration has folded before pressure from Senator Patrick Leahy who is blocking appropriated funds for helicopters needed in Mexico. Apprehending the criminal leadership and protecting threatened law enforcement personnel across the extensive territory south of our border requires rapid airlift. Delay costs more Mexican lives.

Medical Marijuana and Mexican Mafias

On the key issue of illegal drugs—the widely recognized source of criminal power in Mexico—the Obama administration is lurching dangerously in reverse. In his first statement on drug policy, Attorney General Eric Holder suggested he may no longer enforce federal law against trafficking marijuana if the traffickers call their marijuana medical. Both U.S. and Mexican officials at all levels know that medical marijuana is an utter fraud used to undermine drug enforcement in the United States. Mexican officials also know (as does the Justice Department) that much of the marijuana sold in the "dispensaries" of California funds the mafias of Mexico.

Marijuana sales are the single largest source of drug profits for these criminals—on top of funds from kidnapping, protection rackets, alien smuggling, and car theft. Not enforcing our marijuana laws makes these terrorists stronger. Pretending to take legalization seriously makes them stronger still.

What do we think the brave officers risking their lives in Mexico feel when our attorney general sounds like he is going to do less to help? Is it too much to expect him to make clear that enforcing our marijuana laws reduces addiction here and saves lives in Mexico?

The U.S. Drug Czar

And what must Mexican officials think about Vice President [Joe] Biden's recent announcement that the next director of drug control policy would be kicked out of the Obama cabinet?

It was Joe Biden who complained over and over again when the first director, Bill Bennett, was not made a member of the elder President [George H.W.] Bush's cabinet. Biden told Bennett his work would necessarily be viewed as lesser than that of other senior officials. His point was you can talk, but you cannot be as strong within the administration without being at that table. I served with Bill Bennett and I was a member of the cabinet in the last administration—Joe Biden was right. Continuing our sharp reductions in use and supply require strong management, effectively shaping drug control programs in almost every executive department. Everyone in Washington knows rank is a part of strength.

The failure of President Obama to announce the new director himself, coupled with the demotion from cabinet membership, indicates two things. There must have been an internal debate over something the vice president cares very much about and he lost. More importantly, it shows that President Obama is not committed and that is dangerous for Mexico and the United States.

I hope that this will change. The recently released *Forbes* list of wealthiest people in the world includes one of Mexico's most dangerous criminal leaders. President Obama should make it his goal to help President Calderón apprehend this man and those like him as soon as possible.

Organizations to Contact

The editors have compiled the following list of organizations concerned with the issues debated in this book. The descriptions are derived from materials provided by the organizations. All have publications or information available for interested readers. The list was compiled on the date of publication of the present volume; the information provided here may change. Be aware that many organizations take several weeks or longer to respond to inquiries, so allow as much time as possible.

American Alliance for Medical Cannabis (AAMC)
44500 Tide Avenue, Arch Cape, OR   97102
(503) 436-1882
e-mail: contact@letfreedomgrow.com
website: www.letfreedomgrow.com

American Alliance for Medical Cannabis (AAMC) is dedicated to bringing patients, caregivers, and volunteers the facts they need to make informed decisions about medical marijuana. AAMC advocates for the rights of medical marijuana patients through education and interaction with government representatives. AAMC provides literature on the common medical uses of marijuana on its website.

American Civil Liberties Union (ACLU)
125 Broad Street, 18th Floor, New York, NY   10004
(212) 549-2500
e-mail: aclu@aclu.org
website: www.aclu.org

The American Civil Liberties Union (ACLU) is a national organization that works to defend Americans' civil rights guaranteed by the US Constitution by providing legal defense, research, and education. The ACLU opposes the criminal prohibition of marijuana and the civil liberties violations that result from it. The ACLU Drug Law Reform Project engages in campaigns and submits briefs in relevant law cases. Literature about these campaigns and text of the briefs are available on the ACLU's website.

Americans for Safe Access (ASA)

1322 Webster Street, Suite 402, Oakland, CA   94612
(510) 251-1856 • fax: (510) 251-2036
e-mail: info@safeaccessnow.org
website: www.safeaccessnow.org

Americans for Safe Access (ASA) is an organization of patients, medical professionals, scientists, and concerned citizens promoting safe and legal access to marijuana for therapeutic use and research. ASA works to overcome political and legal barriers by creating policies that improve access to medical cannabis for patients and researchers through legislation, education, litigation, grassroots actions, advocacy, and services for patients and their caregivers. ASA publishes booklets, which are available on its website, about the use of cannabis for medical conditions.

Cato Institute

1000 Massachusetts Avenue NW
Washington, DC   20001-5403
(202) 842-0200 • fax: (202) 842-3490
e-mail: cato@cato.org
website: www.cato.org

The Cato Institute is a public policy research foundation dedicated to limiting the control of government and to protecting individual liberty. The Cato Institute strongly favors drug legalization. The institute publishes the *Cato Journal* three times a year and the *Cato Policy Report* bimonthly.

Center for Medicinal Cannabis Research (CMCR)

220 Dickinson Street, Suite B, Mail Code 8231
San Diego, CA   92103-8231
(619) 543-5024

e-mail: cmcr@ucsd.edu

website: www.cmcr.ucsd.edu

Center for Medicinal Cannabis Research (CMCR) conducts scientific studies intended to ascertain the general medical safety and efficacy of cannabis and cannabis products. CMCR aims to be a resource for health policy planning on the issue of medical marijuana. CMCR provides a list of its published research on its website, with access to select publications.

Drug Free America Foundation Inc. (DFAF)

5999 Central Avenue, Suite 301, Saint Petersburg, FL 33710

(727) 828-0211 • fax: (727) 828-0212

website: www.dfaf.org

Drug Free America Foundation Inc. (DFAF) is a drug prevention and policy organization committed to developing, promoting, and sustaining global strategies, policies, and laws that will reduce illegal drug use, drug addiction, drug-related injury, and death. DFAF opposes efforts that would legalize, decriminalize, or promote illicit drugs, including the legalization of medical marijuana. DFAF publishes several position statements, including "Marijuana—Questions and Answers," which are available on its website.

Drug Policy Alliance (DPA)

70 West Thirty-sixth Street, 16th Floor, New York, NY 10018

(212) 613-8020 • fax: (212) 613-8021

e-mail: nyc@drugpolicy.org

website: www.drugpolicy.org

Drug Policy Alliance (DPA) supports and publicizes alternatives to current US policies on illegal drugs, including marijuana. DPA has worked on initiatives in several states to make medical marijuana legally available to ill patients. DPA publishes many research briefs and fact sheets, such as "Medical Marijuana and Cancer," which are available on its website.

Marijuana Policy Project (MPP)

236 Massachusetts Avenue NE, Suite 400
Washington, DC   20002
(202) 462-5747
e-mail: info@mpp.org
website: www.mpp.org

Marijuana Policy Project (MPP) works to further public policies that allow for responsible medical and nonmedical use of marijuana and that minimize the harms associated with marijuana consumption and the laws that manage its use. MPP works to increase public support for marijuana regulation and lobbies for marijuana policy reform at the state and federal levels. MPP works to increase public awareness through speaking engagements, educational seminars, the mass media, and briefing papers.

National Institute on Drug Abuse (NIDA)

National Institutes of Health, 6001 Executive Boulevard
Room 5213, Bethesda, MD   20892-9561
(301) 443-1124
e-mail: information@nida.nih.gov
website: www.nida.nih.gov

National Institute on Drug Abuse (NIDA) is a part of the National Institutes of Health, a component of the US Department of Health and Human Services, with the mission of using science to address drug abuse and addiction. NIDA supports and conducts research on drug abuse—including the yearly Monitoring the Future survey—to improve addiction prevention, treatment, and policy efforts. It publishes the bimonthly *NIDA Notes* newsletter, the periodic *NIDA Capsules* fact sheets, and a catalog of research reports and public education materials, including *Marijuana: Facts for Teens* and *Marijuana: Facts Parents Need to Know.*

National Organization for the Reform of Marijuana Laws (NORML)

1600 K Street NW, Suite 501, Washington, DC   20006-2832
(202) 483-5500 • fax: (202) 483-0057
e-mail: norml@norml.org
website: www.norml.org

The mission of the National Organization for the Reform of Marijuana Laws (NORML) is to move public opinion to achieve the repeal of marijuana prohibition so that the responsible use of cannabis by adults is no longer subject to penalty. NORML lobbies state and federal legislators in support of reform legislation, including the end of marijuana prohibition for both medical and personal use. NORML has numerous research and position papers available on its website, including "Cannabis, Mental Health, and Context: The Case For Regulation."

Office of National Drug Control Policy (ONDCP)

Drug Policy Information Clearinghouse, PO Box 6000
Rockville, MD   20849-6000
(800) 666-3332 • fax: (301) 519-5212
e-mail: ondcp@ncjrs.org
website: www.whitehousedrugpolicy.gov

The Office of National Drug Control Policy (ONDCP), a component of the Executive Office of the President, establishes policies, priorities, and objectives for the nation's drug control program. ONDCP works to reduce illicit drug use, manufacturing, and trafficking; drug-related crime and violence; and drug-related health consequences. ONDCP has numerous publications related to its mission, including *Marijuana Myths & Facts: The Truth Behind 10 Popular Misperceptions.*

Bibliography

Books

Arthur Benavie | *Drugs: America's Holy War.* New York: Routledge, 2009.

Richard Glen Boire and Kevin Feeney | *Medical Marijuana Law.* Ed. Beverly A. Potter. Berkeley, CA: Ronin, 2006.

Martin Booth | *Cannabis: A History.* New York: Picador, 2005.

Wendy Chapkis and Richard J. Webb | *Dying to Get High: Marijuana as Medicine.* New York: New York University Press, 2008.

Mitch Earlywine, ed. | *Pot Politics: Marijuana and the Costs of Prohibition.* New York: Oxford University Press, 2007.

Madelon Lubin Finkel | *Truth, Lies, and Public Health: How We Are Affected When Science and Politics Collide.* Westport, CT: Praeger, 2007.

Steve Fox, Paul Armentano, and Mason Tvert | *Marijuana Is Safer: So Why Are We Driving People to Drink?* White River Junction, VT: Chelsea Green Publishing, 2009.

John Geluardi | *Cannabiz: The Explosive Rise of the Medical Marijuana Industry.* Sausalito, CA: Polipoint Press, 2010.

| Joseph W. Jacob | *Medical Uses of Marijuana.* Bloomington, IN: Trafford, 2009. |

Albert T. Johnson, ed. — *Medical Marijuana and Marijuana Use.* New York: Nova Science, 2009.

Stephen A. Maisto, Mark Galizio, and Gerard J. Connors — *Drug Use and Abuse.* Belmont, CA: Wadsworth/Cengage, 2010.

Robin Room, Benedikt Fischer, Wayne Hall, Simon Lenton, and Peter Reuter — *Cannabis Policy: Moving Beyond Stalemate.* New York: Oxford University Press, 2010.

Periodicals

Baltimore Sun — "Marijuana Conundrum," February 1, 2010.

Doug Bandow — "Arrest Michael Phelps Now!" *National Review Online*, February 6, 2009. www.nationalreview.com.

Tom Barnidge — "If Government Doesn't Control Marijuana, Criminals Will," *Contra Costa Times* (Contra Costa, CA), January 23, 2010.

Michael Brannigan — "Let the Sick Decide if Marijuana Is Medicine," *Times Union* (Albany, NY), March 28, 2010.

Joseph A. Califano Jr. — "Should Drugs Be Decriminalised? No," *British Medical Journal* (*BMJ*), November 10, 2007.

Christian Science Monitor	"Legalize Marijuana? Not So Fast," May 22, 2009.
Jessica Peck Corry	"Republican Moms for Marijuana: 'Time to Legalize Is Now,'" *Colorado Daily*, July 26, 2009.
Dora Dixie and Pete Bensinger	"Medical Marijuana Is Bad Medicine, Bad Policy," *Daily Herald* (Arlington Heights, IL), June 2, 2010.
David M. Fergusson, Joseph M. Boden, and L. John Horwood	"Cannabis Use and Other Illicit Drug Use: Testing the Cannabis Gateway Hypothesis," *Addiction*, April 2006.
Dennis M. Gorman and J. Charles Huber Jr.	"Do Medical Cannabis Laws Encourage Cannabis Use?" *International Journal of Drug Policy*, May 2007.
Lester Grinspoon	"Marijuana as Wonder Drug," *Boston Globe*, March 1, 2007.
Sanjay Gupta	"Why I Would Vote No on Pot," *Time*, January 8, 2009.
Diane E. Hoffman and Ellen Weber	"Medical Marijuana and the Law," *New England Journal of Medicine*, April 22, 2010.
Gary Johnson	"Legalize Pot to Cut Crime, Fill Coffers," *Sacramento Bee*, June 22, 2010.
Tim Lynch and Juan Carlos Hidalgo	"Get Serious About Decriminalizing Drugs; Others Are," *San Jose Mercury News*, September 29, 2009.

Bruce Mirken   "The Case for Medical Marijuana,"
                      Forbes, August 21, 2009.

Jeffrey A. Miron   "Legalize Drugs to Stop Violence,"
                      CNN.com, March 24, 2009.
                      www.cnn.com.

New York Times   "The Politics of Pot," April 22, 2006.

Kathleen Parker   "Phelps Takes a Hit," *Washington
                      Post*, February 4, 2009.

John Stossel   "Legalize All Drugs," *Jewish World
                      Review*, June 18, 2008.

Kelley Beaucar   "Higher Law: Will States' Rights Go
Vlahos   Up in Smoke?" *American
                      Conservative*, March 9, 2009.

Ray Warren   "Because Marijuana Eradication
                      Policy Is Hopeless, Tax and Regulate
                      Instead," *Los Angeles Daily Journal*,
                      July 19, 2007.

Index